grzimek's
Student Animal Life Resource

• • • •

grzimek's
Student Animal Life Resource

• • • •

Reptiles
volume 2

Night lizards to Cobras, Kraits, and their Relatives

Leslie A. Mertz, PhD, author

Madeline S. Harris, project editor
Neil Schlager and Jayne Weisblatt, editors

Detroit • New York • San Francisco • San Diego • New Haven, Conn. • Waterville, Maine • London • Munich

Grzimek's Student Animal Life Resource: Reptiles

Leslie A. Mertz, PhD

Project Editor
Madeline S. Harris

Editorial
Kathleen J. Edgar, Melissa Hill, Heather Price

Indexing Services
Synapse, the Knowledge Link Corporation

Rights and Acquisitions
Sheila Spencer, Mari Masalin-Cooper

Imaging and Multimedia
Randy Bassett, Michael Logusz, Dan Newell, Chris O'Bryan, Robyn Young

Product Design
Tracey Rowens, Jennifer Wahi

Composition
Evi Seoud, Mary Beth Trimper

Manufacturing
Wendy Blurton, Dorothy Maki

LIBRARY OF CONGRESS CATALOGING-IN-PUBLICATION DATA

Mertz, Leslie A.
Grzimek's student animal life resource. Reptiles / Leslie A. Mertz ; edited by Neil Schlager and Jayne Weisblatt.
        p. cm.
   Includes bibliographical references and index.
   ISBN 0-7876-9404-5 (hardcover set : alk. paper) — ISBN 0-7876-9405-3 (volume 1) — ISBN 0-7876-9406-1 (volume 2)
   1. Reptiles—Juvenile literature. I. Schlager, Neil, 1966- II. Weisblatt, Jayne. III. Title.
   QL644.2.M427 2005
   597.9—dc22   2005000033

ISBN 0-7876-9402-9 (21-vol set), ISBN 0-7876-9404-5 (2-vol set), ISBN 0-7876-9405-3 (vol 1), ISBN 0-7876-9406-1 (vol 2)

This title is also available as an e-book
Contact your Thomson Gale sales representative for ordering information.

Printed in Canada
10 9 8 7 6 5 4 3 2 1

Contents

Reader's Guide

Grzimek's Student Animal Life Resource: Reptiles offers readers comprehensive and easy-to-use information on Earth's reptiles. Order entries provide an overview of a group of families, and family entries provide an overview of a particular family. Entries are arranged by taxonomy, the science through which living things are classified into related groups. Each entry includes sections on physical characteristics; geographic range; habitat; diet; behavior and reproduction; animals and people; and conservation status. All entries are followed by one or more species accounts with the same information as well as a range map and photo or illustration for each species. Entries conclude with a list of books, periodicals, and Web sites that may be used for further research.

ADDITIONAL FEATURES

Each volume of *Grzimek's Student Animal Life Resource: Reptiles* includes a pronunciation guide for scientific names, a glossary, an overview of Reptiles, a list of species in the set by biome, a list of species by geographic range, and an index. The set has 180 full-color maps, photos, and illustrations to enliven the text, and sidebars provide additional facts and related information.

NOTE

Grzimek's Student Animal Life Resource: Reptiles has standardized information in the Conservation Status section. The IUCN Red List provides the world's most comprehensive inventory of the global conservation status of plants and animals. Using a set of criteria to evaluate extinction risk, the IUCN recognizes the following categories: Extinct, Extinct in the Wild, Critically Endangered, Endangered, Vulnerable, Conservation Dependent, Near Threatened, Least Concern, and Data Deficient. These terms are defined where they are used in the text, but for a complete explanation of each category, visit the IUCN web page at http://www.iucn.org/themes/ssc/redlists/RLcats2001booklet.html.

ACKNOWLEDGEMENTS

Gale would like to thank several individuals for their assistance with this set. Leslie Mertz wrote the vast majority of the text; Linda Patricia Kite also wrote a few articles. At Schlager Group Inc., Neil Schlager and Jayne Weisblatt coordinated the writing and editing of the set, while Marcia Merryman Means and Leah Tieger also provided valuable assistance.

Special thanks are also due for the invaluable comments and suggestions provided by the *Grzimek's Student Animal Life Resource: Reptiles* advisors:

- Mary Alice Anderson, Media Specialist, Winona Middle School, Winona, Minnesota
- Thane Johnson, Librarian, Oklahoma City Zoo, Oklahoma City, Oklahoma
- Debra Kachel, Media Specialist, Ephrata Senior High School, Ephrata, Pennsylvania
- Nina Levine, Media Specialist, Blue Mountain Middle School, Courtlandt Manor, New York
- Ruth Mormon, Media Specialist, The Meadows School, Las Vegas, Nevada

COMMENTS AND SUGGESTIONS

We welcome your comments on *Grzimek's Student Animal Life Resource: Reptiles* and suggestions for future editions of this work. Please write: Editors, *Grzimek's Student Animal Life Resource: Reptiles*, U•X•L, 27500 Drake Rd., Farmington Hills, Michigan 48331-3535; call toll free: 1-800-877-4253; fax: 248-699-8097; or send e-mail via www.gale.com.

Pronunciation Guide for Scientific Names

Acanthophis antarcticus uh-KAN-thuh-fuhs ant-ARK-tih-kuhs

Acrochordidae AK-ruh-KOR-duh-dee

Acrochordus granulatus AK-ruh-KOR-duhs GRAN-yoo-LAH-tuhs

Agama hispida uh-GAM-uh HIH-spih-duh

Agamidae uh-GAM-uh-dee

Agamodon anguliceps uh-GAM-uh-don AN-guh-LIH-seps

Agkistrodon piscivorus ag-KIS-truh-DON PIH-sih-VER-uhs

Alligator mississippiensis AL-uh-GAY-der MIS-uh-SIP-ee-EN-suhs

Alligatoridae AL-uh-guh-TOR-uh-dee

Amphisbaena alba AM-fus-BEE-nuh AL-buh

Amphisbaenidae AM-fus-BEE-nuh-dee

Anguidae ANG-gwuh-dee

Aniliidae AN-uh-LY-uh-dee

Anilius scytale AN-uh-LY-uhs SY-tuh-lee

Anolis carolinensis uh-NOH-luhs kar-uh-LINE-en-sis

Anomalepididae uh-NOM-uh-luh-PID-uh-dee

Anomochilidae AN-uh-moh-KIL-uh-dee

Anomochilus leonardi AN-uh-moh-KIL-uhs LEE-oh-nar-DY

Apalone spinifera uh-PAL-uh-nee SPIH-nih-FER-uh

Aspidites melanocephalus a-SPID-uh-teez MEL-uh-noh-SEF-uh-luhs

Atractaspididae at-TRAK-tuh-SPID-uh-dee

Atractaspis bibronii at-TRAK-tuh-spuhs bib-ROH-nee-EYE

Bachia bresslaui buh-KEE-uh BREZ-lou-eye

Bipedidae by-PED-uh-dee

Bipes biporus BY-peez by-POR-uhs

Boa constrictor constrictor BOH-uh kun-STRIK-ter kun-STRIK-ter

Boidae BOH-uh-dee

Bolyeriidae boh-LY-uh-REE-uh-dee

Brookesia perarmata broo-KEEZ-ee-uh per-ARM-uh-tuh

Caiman crocodilus KAY-mun KRAH-kuh-DIL-uhs

Cape ctenosaura hemilopha KAYP STEN-uh-SOR-uh heh-MIL-uh-fuh

Caretta caretta kuh-RED-uh kuh-RED-uh

Carettochelyidae kuh-RED-oh-kuh-LY-uh-dee

Carettochelys insculpta kuh-RED-oh-KUH-leez in-SKULP-tuh

Casarea dussumieri KAY-suh-REE-uh duh-SOO-mee-AIR-eye

Cerastes cerastes suh-ROS-teez suh-ROS-teez

Chamaeleo chamaeleon kuh-MEE-lee-OH kuh-MEE-lee-ON

Chamaeleo jacksonii kuh-MEE-lee-OH JAK-suh-NEE-eye

Chamaeleonidae kuh-MEE-lee-ON-uh-dee

Chelidae KEL-uh-dee

Chelonia mydas kuh-LON-ee-uh MY-duhs

Cheloniidae KEL-uh-NY-uh-dee

Chelus fimbriatus KEL-uhs fim-bree-AH-tuhs

Chelydra serpentina kuh-LIH-druh ser-pen-TEE-nuh

Chelydridae kuh-LIH-druh-dee

Chlamydosaurus kingii kluh-MID-uh-SOR-uhs KIN-jee-eye

Chrysemys picta KRY-suh-meez PIK-tuh

Cistoclemmys flavomarginata sis-TOK-luh-meez FLAV-uh-MAR-gih-NAH-tuh

Cnemidophorus sexlineatus snuh-MID-uh-FOR-uhs SEKS-lih-NEE-ah-tuhs

Coleonyx variegates KOH-lee-ON-iks VAIR-ee-uh-GAH-teez

Colubridae kuh-LOO-bruh-dee

Corallus caninus koh-RAL-is kay-NINE-uhs

Cordylidae kor-DIL-uh-dee

Curucia zebrata kuh-ROO-shee-uh zee-BRAH-tuh

Crocodilians KRAH-kuh-DIL-ee-unz

Crocodilurus lacertinus KRAH-kuh-DIL-oor-uhs luh-SER-duh-nuhs

Crocodylidae KRAH-kuh-DIL-uh-dee

Crocodylus acutus KRAH-kuh-DIL-uhs uh-KYOO-tuhs

Crocodylus niloticus KRAH-kuh-DIL-uhs NY-lah-TIH-kuhs
Crotalus horridus KROH-tuh-luhs hoh-RID-uhs
Cylindrophiidae suh-LIN-druh-FEE-uh-dee
Cylindrophis rufus suh-LIN-druh-FIS ROO-fuhs
Dermatemydidae DER-muh-tuh-MID-uh-DEE
Dermatemys mawii der-muh-TEH-mis muh-WEE-eye
Dermochelyidae DER-muh-kuh-LY-uh-dee
Dermochelys coriacea DER-muh-KEL-eez KOH-ree-ah-SEE-uh
Dibamidae dy-BAH-muh-dee
Dibamus bourreti dy-BAH-muhs BOOR-uh-ty
Dispholidus typus DIS-fuh-LEE-duhs TY-puhs
Draco volans DRAY-koh VOH-lunz
Drymarchon corais DRIH-mar-kun KOR-ray
Elapidae uh-LOP-uh-dee
Emydidae uh-MID-uh-dee
Eumeces laticeps YOO-muh-seez LAD-ih-seps
Eunectes murinus yoo-NEK-teez myoo-REE-nuhs
Gavialidae GAY-vee-AL-uh-dee
Gavialis gangeticus GAY-vee-AL-is gan-JET-uh-kuhs
Gekkonidae geh-KON-uh-dee
Geochelone nigra JEE-oh-KEL-uh-nee NIG-ruh
Geoemydidae JEE-oh-uh-MID-uh-dee
Gerrhonotus liocephalus JER-uh-NOH-duhs LEE-oh-SEF-uh-luhs
Gopherus agassizii go-FER-uhs AG-uh-SEE-zee-eye
Gymnophthalmidae JIM-noh-THAL-muh-dee
Heloderma suspectum HEE-loh-DER-muh suh-SPEK-tum
Helodermatidae HEE-loh-der-MAD-uh-dee
Hemidactylus frenatus HEM-uh-DAK-tih-luhs FREH-nah-tuhs
Heterodon platyrhinos HED-uh-ROH-don PLAD-ih-RY-nohs
Iguanidae ih-GWON-uh-dee
Kinosternidae KIH-nuh-STER-nuh-dee
Lacerta agilis luh-SER-duh uh-JIL-uhs
Lacertidae luh-SER-duh-dee
Lachesis melanocephala luh-KEE-suhs MEL-uh-noh-SEF-uh-luh
Lampropeltis triangulum LAMP-roh-PEL-tuhs TRY-ang-YOO-lum
Laticauda colubrina luh-TIK-oh-duh kuh-LOO-bree-nuh
Leptotyphlopidae LEP-toh-ty-FLOP-uh-dee

Leptotyphlops dulcis LEP-toh-TY-flops DUL-sis

Liotyphlops ternetzii LEE-uh-TY-flops ter-NET-zee-EYE

Loxocemidae LOK-suh-SEM-uh-dee

Loxocemus bicolor LOK-suh-SEM-uhs BY-kuh-ler

Micrurus fulvius my-KRER-uhs ful-VEE-uhs

Morelia viridis moh-REEL-ee-uh vih-RID-is

Naja nigricollis NAH-juh NIH-grih-KOHL-luhs

Ophiophagus hannah ah-FEE-ah-fuh-guhs HAN-nuh

Pelomedusa subrufa puh-LOM-uh-DOO-suh SUB-ruh-fuh

Pelomedusidae puh-LOM-uh-DOO-suh-dee

Platysaurus capensis PLAT-ih-SOR-uhs KAY-pen-sis

Platysternidae PLAT-ih-STER-nuh-dee

Platysternon megacephalum PLAT-ih-STER-nun MEG-uh-SEF-uh-lum

Plectrurus perrotetii plek-TRER-uhs PAIR-uh-TET-ee-eye

Podocnemididae poh-DOK-nuh-MID-uh-dee

Podocnemis expansa poh-DOK-nuh-MIS ek-SPAN-suh

Python reticulatus PY-thon ruh-TIK-yoo-LAH-tuhs

Pythonidae PY-thon-uh-dee

Ramphotyphlops nigrescens RAM-fuh-TY-flops nih-GRES-unz

Rhineura floridana ry-NYOOR-uh floh-RID-uh-nuh

Rhineuridae ry-NYOOR-uh-dee

Sauromalus obesus soh-ROM-uh-luhs oh-BEE-suhs

Scincidae SKIN-kuh-DEE

Scincus scincus SKIN-kuhs SKIN-kuhs

Sphenodon punctatus SFEN-uh-don PUNK-tah-tuhs

Sphenodontidae SFEN-uh-DON-tuh-dee

Squamata skwuh-MOD-uh

Sternotherus odoratus STER-nah-THUH-ruhs OH-duh-RAH-tuhs

Teiidae TEE-uh-dee

Terrapene carolina ter-ROP-uh-nee KAR-uh-LINE-uh

Testudines tes-TYOO-duh-neez

Testudinidae TES-tyoo-DIN-uh-dee

Thamnophis sirtalis THAM-nuh-FIS ser-TAL-is

Trionychidae TRY-un-NIK-uh-dee

Trogonophidae TROG-uh-NOH-fuh-dee

Tropidophiidae TROP-uh-doh-FEE-uh-dee

Typhlopidae ty-FLOP-uh-dee

Ungaliophis panamensis un-GALL-ee-OH-fis PAN-uh-MEN-sis

Uropeltidae YOOR-uh-PEL-tuh-dee

Varanidae vuh-RAN-uh-dee

Varanus salvadorii vuh-RAN-uhs SAL-vuh-DOR-ee-EYE

Viperidae VY-per-uh-dee

Xantusia vigilis ZAN-tuh-SEE-uh vih-JUH-lis

Xantusiidae ZAN-tuh-SEE-uh-dee

Xenopeltidae ZEE-noh-PELT-uh-dee

Xenopeltis unicolor ZEE-noh-PELT-uhs YOO-nih-KUH-ler

Xenosauridae ZEE-noh-SOR-uh-dee

Xenosaurus grandis ZEE-noh-SOR-uhs GRAN-duhs

Words to Know

A

Algae: Tiny plantlike growths that live in water and have no true roots, stems, or leaves.

Ambush: A method of hunting in which the animal finds a hiding place from which it can spring out to attack unsuspecting meal animals that wander past.

Amphibian: An animal with a skeleton inside the body and that spends part of its life in the water and part on land.

Amphisbaenians: A small group of reptiles that look somewhat like long earthworms, but with scales.

Annuli: Rings, such as those seen around the length of an earthworm and some wormlizards.

Antibodies: Substances that fight bacteria, which can cause health problems in humans.

Antivenin: An antidote, or remedy, that neutralizes, or makes ineffective, the poison from the bite of a venomous animal.

Arboreal: Describing an animal living in trees.

Arid: Describing areas with very little water, such as a desert area.

Autohemorrhaging: Bleeding that starts on its own and not because of an injury.

B

Barbel: A bit of flesh that dangles from the chins of some turtles.

Bask: To warm up the body, especially by lying in the sun; basking is seen in such animals as turtles and snakes.

Bay: A part of the sea that cuts into the coastline.

Billabong: An Australian word for a dried-up streambed.

Blunt: Not pointed.

Brittle: Easily broken.

Bromeliad: A plant that often grows high above the ground on the sides of trees.

Burrow: A tunnel or hole in the ground made by an animal for shelter.

C

Caecilians: Salamanderlike animals that live underground.

Camouflage: A way of hiding or disguising something by making it look like its surroundings.

Carapace: The upper shell of a turtle.

Carnivore: An animal that eats meat.

Carnivorous: Meat-eating.

Carrion: Dead animal flesh.

Caruncle: The toothlike part a hatchling reptile uses to break out of its egg.

Centipede: An animal with a segmented, wormlike body and many legs.

Clone: An exact duplicate, seen in a mother and her babies of parthenogenic species.

Cloud forest: A wet, tropical, mountain forest.

Clutch: A nest of eggs.

Cold-blooded: Having a body temperature that changes with the temperature of the surrounding environment.

Concave: Hollowed or curved inward.

Coniferous forest: A forest with trees that have seeds inside cones, such as pines; also called evergreen forest.

Constriction: A method snakes use to kill their prey, by wrapping their bodies around the prey animal and squeezing until it cannot breathe.

Constrictor: A snake that squeezes animals, usually to death, before eating them.

Continent: A large mass of land on planet Earth, such as Africa or South America.

Continental shelf: A shallow plain in the sea that forms the border of a continent, usually with a steep slope to the ocean floor.

Courtship: An animal's activities that are meant to attract a mate.

Crest: A ridge on an animal's body.

Crepuscular: Describing an animal active at twilight, that is, at dusk and dawn.

Crevice: A narrow opening or a crack.

Critically Endangered: Facing an extremely high risk of extinction in the wild in the near future.

Crustacean: An animal that lives in water and has a soft, segmented body covered by a hard shell, such as lobsters and shrimp.

D

Decayed: Rotting.

Deciduous forest: A forest with trees, such as maples, that lose their leaves in dry or cold weather.

Deflate: To cause to collapse by letting out the air.

Deforestation: Clearing land of trees to use the timber or make room for human settlement or farming.

Depression: A hollow or a hole.

Dew: Small drops of water that collect on cool surfaces, especially at night.

Dewlap: The flap of skin that lies under the chin.

Diameter: The width of a circle, measured as a straight line through the center.

Diurnal: Describing an animal active during the day.

Drought: A dry spell.

Dune: A hill of sand piled up by wind or water.

E

Ectothermic: Describing an animal whose body temperature changes when the outside air warms up or cools down; often referred to as "cold-blooded."

Eggs: The reproductive cells that are made by female animals and that are fertilized by sperm, or reproductive cells of male animals.

Embryo: A developing baby that is not yet born.

Endangered: Facing a very high risk of extinction in the wild in the near future.

Endothermic: Describing an animal that uses its own energy to maintain a constant body temperature; often referred to as "warm-blooded."

Equator: The imaginary circle around Earth midway between the North Pole and the South Pole, the points on Earth's surface that are farthest north and south, respectively.

Erosion: The wearing away of earth by wind or water.

Estivation: A period of inactivity during dry spells or during the summer.

Estuary: The wide part at the lower end of a river, where the river meets the sea.

Evolution: The process of change and development that an animal undergoes over time to adapt to its surroundings.

Extinct: No longer alive.

Extinction: Elimination or death, especially of an entire species of animal.

F

Fangs: Long, pointed teeth.

Flexible: Movable or bendable.

Forage: A style of hunting in which an animal wanders about looking for food.

Fossil: The remains, or parts, of animals that lived long ago, usually found set into rock or earth.

Fossorial species: Those that live underground.

Frill: Pleated or ruffled neck folds.

Fused: Firmly joined together.

G

Genus: Defined by scientists, a group of similar species. A group of similar genera (the plural of genus) make up a family.

Granular: Grainy like sand.

Grub: A wormlike young insect.

H

Habitat: The natural environment, or living area, of an animal.

Hatchling: A newly hatched young animal.

Herbivore: An animal that eats only plants.

Hibernate: Become inactive during the winter.

Hibernation: A period of inactivity during the winter.

Humus: A material made up of decayed, or rotting, plants and leaves that feeds soil and holds in water.

Hybrid: Young born to parents from two different species.

Hydrozoan: An ocean-living animal that has tentacles, or long thin body parts used for feeling or holding on to things.

Hyoid: A bone that supports the tongue.

I

Incubation: The period of time after eggs are laid and before they hatch, during which they develop.

Inflate: To make larger or expand.

Infrared vision: The ability to detect, or to "see," heat.

Invertebrate: An animal, such as an insect, spider, or earthworm, that lacks a backbone.

Iridescent: Having the ability to turn light into many colors, much as rain can bend the sunlight into a rainbow; reflecting different colors depending on the light.

Iridescent scale: Seen in a few snakes, scales that shine different colors depending on how the light hits them.

J

Jacobson's organ: Common in reptiles, an organ that connects to the roof of the mouth by a small opening, called a duct, and helps the animal to smell chemical odors picked up by the tongue.

Juvenile: A young animal.

K

Keel: A ridge on the upper shell of a turtle.

Keeled scale: On a snake, a scale with a ridge down the middle.

L

Lagoon: A shallow body of saltwater near the sea.

Larva: In many insects, such as beetles and butterflies, the life stage after the egg and before the pupa.

Ligament: Tough but flexible tissue that connects bones.

Limbs: Legs.

Lineage: A group of animals that connect species through time to their ancestors.

Live-bearing species: A species, or kind, of animal in which the females give birth to babies rather than laying eggs.

M

Mangrove: A tropical tree or shrub that forms thick growths along coastlines.

Marine: Having to do with the sea.

Migrate: To move from one area or climate to another to breed or feed.

Migration: Movement from one region or climate to another, usually for breeding or feeding.

Mimicry: Resemblance of one usually dangerous species by another usually harmless one.

Mollusk: An animal with a soft, unsegmented body usually covered by a shell, such as a snail or a clam.

Molt: As seen in snakes, the shedding of the outer skin.

Murky: Dim or dark.

Musky: Smelling earthy and sometimes stinky, like the spray of a skunk.

N

Native: Natural to a country, that is, produced by nature and not produced or brought in by humans.

Near Threatened: At risk of becoming threatened with extinction in the future.

Nocturnal: Describing an animal active at night.

Nostrils: Nose holes.

O

Omnivore: An animal that eats both plants and meat.

Omnivorous: Describing an animal that eats both plants and meat.

Opportunistic: Taking advantage of what is available, as in feeding on whatever food can be found.

Opportunistic hunters: Animals that will eat almost anything they happen upon if they are hungry.

Oscillation: In spade-headed wormlizards, the back-and-forth swiveling motion of the head that digs through the soil and forms the smooth sides of the tunnel.

Osteoderms: Bony plates that lie under the surface of the scaly skin in some reptiles, including crocodilians.

Oviparous: Describing an animal that produces and lays shelled eggs that later hatch into young.

Ovoviviparous: Describing a female that produces eggs that hatch inside her body just before she gives birth to the young.

P

Palate: A bony plate on the roof of the mouth.

Parthenogenesis: A type of reproduction where a female can have babies by herself without a male.

Parthenogenic species: An all-female species in which a female can become pregnant and have young by herself and without a male.

Pectoral: Relating to the chest area.

Plastron: The lower shell of a turtle.

Pollution: Poison, waste, or other material that makes the environment dirty and harmful to the health of living things.

Predator: An animal that hunts and kills other animals for food.

Prey: An animal hunted and caught for food.

Protrude: To stick out.

Pupa: In many insects, such as beetles and butterflies, the life stage after the larva and before the adult.

Pupil: The part of the eye through which light passes.

R

Rainforest: A tropical woodland area of evergreen trees that has heavy rainfall all year long.

Range: The area where an animal roams and feeds.

Retract: To pull backward.

Rodent: A small animal, such as a mouse, beaver, or hamster, with long front teeth that it uses for gnawing.

S

Sac: A pouch.

Sandbar: A ridge of sand built up by currents, or the flowing movement of water.

Savanna: A flat plain covered with grass and a few trees.

Scale: A clear, thin film or coating over the eyes or a flat, rigid plate that acts as part of a body covering.

Scent: The particular smell of an animal, which can be left on the surface over which it travels.

School: A large number of fish or other water-dwelling animals that swim together.

Scrub: A flat, dry area of land with small bushes.

Scrubland: Land covered with small bushes.

Scute: A bony or horny scale or plate.

Seasonal: Happening as part of the changes at the different times of the year.

Serpentine locomotion: Seen in snakes and legless lizards, the way they slither in an S-shaped motion.

Setae: Tiny hairs or hairlike projections.

Silt: Fine, tiny specks of earth that settle out of water or fall to the bottom.

Snout: Nose area, usually long and pointed.

Sockets: Hollow openings, usually where one body part fits into another.

Species: A group of animals that share many traits and can mate and produce young with one another.

Spectacle: A see-through scale that covers the eye; seen in snakes and some lizards that do not have blinking eyelids.

Sperm: The reproductive cells that are made by male animals and that fertilize the eggs of female animals.

Specimen: A single example that is considered typical of a group.

Squamates: The group of animals that includes the lizards, snakes, and wormlizards.

Stalking: A type of hunting in which the predator sneaks up on the prey before attacking.

Stratum corneum: The outer skin that snakes lose when they shed.

Subspecies: A smaller group within a species that typically lives in a particular area and usually has a slightly different look from the rest of the animals in the species.

Subtropical: Relating to regions that border on the tropics.

Swamp: A wetland that is only partly or now and then covered by water.

T

Tail: In snakes, the part of the body that occurs after the vent.

Temperate climate: Describing areas that have distinct seasons, including cold winters.

Tentacles: Long thin body parts used for feeling or for holding on to things.

Terrestrial: Describing an animal that lives on land.

Territorial: Describing an animal that is protective of a living or breeding area.

Territory: An animal's preferred living area, which is considered off-limits to other animals of the same species.

Toxic: Poisonous.

Trek: A journey, typically one that is long and difficult.

Trunk: In a snake, the portion of the body between the head and the tail.

Tubercles: The cone-shaped bumps on a snake's tail.

V

Venom: Poison, usually injected by snakes, bees, or scorpions by biting or stinging.

Venomous: Poisonous.

Vent: On a snake, a crosswise opening on the belly side and toward the rear of the animal.

Ventrals: In snakes, the scales on the underside of the animal, usually much larger than the scales on the snake's back and sides.

Vertebrate: An animal that has a backbone.

Vertical: Positioned straight up and down.

Vibrate: To move back and forth rapidly.

Viviparous: Describing a female that makes no eggs, but rather provides all of the food for her young through direct connections inside her body and gives birth to live babies.

Vocal: Making sounds.

Vocal cord: Body part used to produce sound.

Vulnerable: Facing a high risk of extinction in the wild.

W

Wetland: Land that is covered with shallow water or that has very wet soil.

Getting to Know Reptiles

REPTILES

Snakes, crocodiles and alligators, lizards, and turtles might not look alike at first glance, but they all share certain features. These animals, plus the tuataras that resemble a cross between a prehistoric dinosaur and a present-day lizard, are reptiles. In all, the world holds 285 species of turtles, 23 crocodiles and alligators, two tuataras, 4,450 lizards, and 2,900 snakes. Scientists suspect that hundreds of other reptile species have yet to be discovered.

Scales

Almost all reptiles have thick tough skin with scales or scutes. Alligators have large heavy rectangular scales covering their bodies, while snakes often have thinner overlapping scales. Most snakes have larger and wider belly scales, which are known as scutes. Even turtles have noticeable scales on the legs and head. These scales and scutes can help protect the reptile from scraping its skin on the ground or from dangerous attacks by other animals that want to eat it. For land-living reptiles, the scales can also keep the body from drying out too quickly. Besides the scales on their legs, turtles also have a different type of scutes. The tops of the upper and lower shell are divided into large pieces, which are also known as scutes.

Reptiles come in many different sizes and colors. Some snakes grow to less than 12 inches (30.5 centimeters) long as adults, while others can reach 25 feet (7.7 meters). Likewise, a whole range of sizes separate the smallest of turtles at just a

few inches (centimeters) long from the largest, which have shells that can reach 8 feet (2.4 meters) in length. Many reptiles have dull drab colors that help them blend into their surroundings, but others are very brightly colored and patterned.

Body temperature

Reptiles are often called cold-blooded animals, but this description is only correct sometimes. A reptile actually changes its body temperature, becoming hotter when the outside temperature is warm, and colder when the outside temperature is cool. In other words, a reptile is only "cold-blooded" on cold days. This changing body temperature is called ectothermy (EK-toe-ther-mee): ecto means outside and thermy refers to the temperature. Reptiles, then, are ectothermic animals. In "warm-blooded" animals, such as human beings, the body has to stay about the same temperature all the time. If a person's body temperature rises or falls more than just a few degrees, he or she can die. For the ectothermic reptiles, however, their body temperatures can swing 20 to 30° F (7 to 13° C)—and sometimes more—in a single day without causing any harm. Because they are ectothermic, reptiles do not have to use their energy to stay warm. Instead, they can simply let the sun warm them up by sunbathing, or basking, on a forest path or the shore of a river or lake. Ectothermy can also have a downside. Reptiles are slower on cooler days or in the cool morning or evening air, which can make them easy prey for attackers. Most reptiles, however, hide themselves away when their bodies start to chill.

Venom

Not all reptiles are venomous, but many snakes and a few lizards are. Venom is a type of toxin, or poison. Venomous snakes generally have two fangs in their upper jaw—sometimes in the front of the mouth and sometimes in back. These fangs usually have grooves that send the venom down the tooth and into the prey. Unlike the snakes, the two venomous lizards, the Gila monster and the Mexican beaded lizard, store their venom in the lower jaw and deliver it through grooves in numerous teeth.

HOW DO REPTILES MOVE?

Walking

Although not all reptiles have legs, many of them do. Crocodiles and alligators, turtles, most lizards, and tuataras can walk on their four legs. Each leg ends in a foot with five or fewer claws. Usually they walk with their legs held out from the body, rather like a human would hold up his or her body when doing a push-up. Many of the smaller lizards, in particular, are very speedy, zipping across the ground at speeds that make their capture difficult. The exceptionally large lizards, known as Komodo dragons, usually walk very slowly, as do crocodiles, which often slide their bellies along the ground while walking. If necessary, however, both can run surprisingly fast. A few reptiles, such as the Nile crocodile and American crocodile, can even do a fast rabbitlike hop, called a gallop, to cover ground quickly. Some lizards can run on just their two hind legs, and the basilisk lizard is even able to run across the surface of a pond without sinking.

Slithering

Snakes slither, usually twisting and bending their bodies in an S-shaped pattern along the ground. This type of movement is called serpentine (SER-pen-teen) locomotion. Like the snakes, some lizards also have no legs. They move much the

FLYING REPTILES?

No reptiles can actually fly, but several can glide through the air much like a paper airplane. The flying tree snake, which is common in Singapore, flattens out its body to soar from one tree branch to a lower one. The common gliding lizard, also known as the common flying dragon, can likewise glide through the air, but it does so by stretching out a large flap of skin, as if opening a fan, on each side of the body. The flying geckos of Southeast Asia have numerous little flaps on their body, tail, legs, and head that help them to glide.

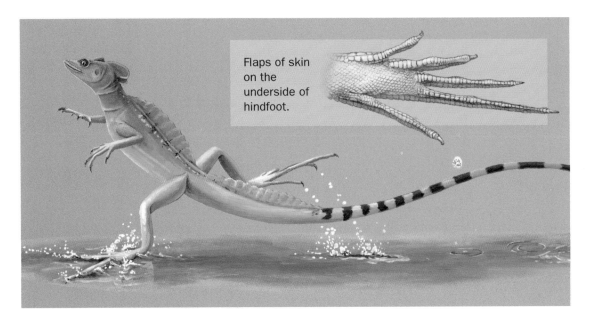

Flaps of skin on the underside of hindfoot.

The green basilisk lizard is able to run across water aided by the flaps of skin on the underside of its hindfeet. (Illustration by Emily Damstra. Reproduced by permission.)

same way as snakes do. Occasionally, some lizards that have legs will slither instead of run. When they are in thick grass that makes running very difficult, some will lie down, hold the legs against the body, and begin to slither.

Swimming

Many turtles, alligators, and crocodiles spend most of their lives in the water. Turtles often have wide feet that they use to push them through the water. A few, like the seaturtles, even

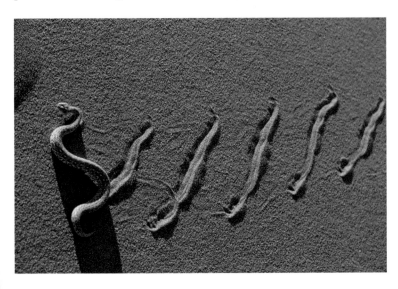

Snakes slither, usually twisting and bending their bodies in an S-shaped pattern along the ground. (David Hughes/Bruce Coleman, Inc. Reproduced by permission.)

have feet that are shaped like paddles. Alligators and crocodiles have very powerful and long tails that propel and steer their bodies through the water. Many snakes are also excellent swimmers, moving through lakes and streams with the same serpentine locomotion they use to slither on land.

WHAT DO REPTILES EAT?

Carnivores

Many reptiles are meat-eaters, or carnivores (KAR-nih-vores). Some of them, especially the smaller lizards and snakes, eat mainly insects, spiders, worms, and other invertebrates (in-VER-teh-brehts), which are animals without backbones. Larger snakes often eat mammals, amphibians, other reptiles, fishes, and birds. A number of snakes and lizards also eat eggs. Snakes usually will only eat living animals, but other species, including snapping turtles, will eat dead, even rotting animals that they find.

Plant eaters

A few reptiles, especially some of the turtle species and a few lizards, eat plants. Animals that eat plants are called herbivores (ER-bih-vores). A few animals will eat both meat and plants. These are called omnivores (OM-nih-vores). Some turtles, including the commonly seen painted turtles, will switch from a mostly meat diet to one that is mostly plants when animal prey are hard to find.

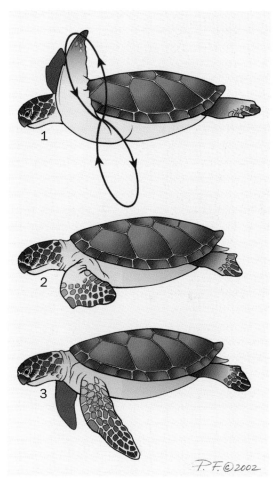

Seaturtle swimming strokes. (Illustration by Patricia Ferrer. Reproduced by permission.)

REPTILES AS PREDATORS AND PREY

As predators

Predators (PREH-duh-ters) are animals that hunt and kill other animals for food. Many reptiles hunt by ambush, which means that they find a good hiding spot or lie very still and wait for a prey animal to happen by. Then they lunge out and grab their prey. Other reptiles hunt by foraging, when they crawl, slither, or swim about looking for something to eat. Many

An Amazon tree boa eating a bird. (Joe McDonald, Bruce Coleman Inc. Reproduced by permission.)

reptiles, including lizards and turtles, simply snap their mouths around the prey and swallow it. Crocodiles and alligators clamp their jaws around larger prey, such as deer, drag them underwater to drown, and then tear off hunks of flesh. Snakes usually swallow their meals whole, often by unhinging their jaws. Many snakes are venomous, which allows them to inject a toxin into the prey to either kill it or knock it out.

Some reptiles, especially the lizards, mainly use their eyes to spot their prey. Snakes have an excellent sense of smell and are able to pick up scents from the air and from the ground with the tongue, which they flick again and again while looking for food. Some snakes, including the pit vipers, have small holes on the front of the face. These holes, or pits, are covered with a thin sheet of detectors that can pick up the heat given off by a prey animal. Snakes are also able to sense ground vibrations through the jaw bone, which connects to the ear. They can not only feel the ground move, but they can also hear it.

As prey

Prey are those animals that are hunted by other animals for food. Eagles, hawks, other large birds, along with some mammals, eat snakes and lizards. In fact, some snakes and lizards eat other snakes and lizards. One of the biggest threats to turtles come from mammals that dig up their nests and eat their eggs.

WHERE REPTILES LIVE

Underground reptiles

The tuataras, many lizards, and some snakes, including the blind snakes, spend most of their time underground in burrows, or beneath rocks, logs, or other ground covers. Some of them stay underground all day and only come out at night. Others stay underground all night and sneak out during the day. Some burrowing reptiles dig their own burrows, but many others simply move into the burrow of another animal.

Freshwater reptiles

Alligators and crocodiles, many turtles, some snakes, and a few lizards live in freshwater lakes, ponds, rivers, and streams. Depending on the species, they may spend a good deal of time every day on shore basking in a sunny spot. Some will even do some hunting on land. Crocodiles, for instance, may grab a prey animal on shore but will then drag it into the water to drown it.

Sea reptiles

Among the reptiles, the seaturtles are most known for their association with the oceans. With their paddlelike front legs, they can glide easily through the water and cover very long distances, often migrating hundreds of miles (kilometers) between their nesting beaches in warm climates and their feeding areas in cooler climates. The leatherback seaturtle migrates the farthest, taking trips of up to 3,100 miles (5,000 kilometers) from its nesting place to a feeding site. Some snakes also live in the ocean. The seasnakes make their home in coral reefs, where they eat eels and fishes.

Tree reptiles

Animals that live in trees are said to be arboreal (pronounced ar-BOR-ee-ul). Some reptiles are arboreal. These include many snakes, even large ones like the emerald tree boa that can grow to 7.3 feet (2.2 meters) in length. Many lizards are also excellent climbers and slither through trees looking for insects or bird eggs to eat.

NEW REPTILES

Scientists believe that many more reptiles live on Earth than those they know about. In fact, they are continuing to find new reptiles today.

Sometimes, they discover new species inside old ones. In other words, they decide that a snake or lizard that they always thought was one species is actually two similar-looking species. In 2003, for example, Wolfgang Waster of the School of Biological Sciences at the University of Wales and keepers from the London Zoo received a group of strangely colored spitting cobras. After taking a closer look, they discovered that the snakes were actually a completely different and previously unknown species, which they called the Nubian cobra. Similarly, zoologist Frank Burbrink studied American corn snakes and found that one was so different from the others that it should be its own species. He named the snake Slowinski's corn snake in honor of snake researcher Joseph Slowinski, who died in 2001 when he was bitten by venomous snake.

Besides finding new species in old ones, scientists are also discovering new never-before-seen species in remote places where few humans have ever traveled. In 2001, for example, scientists Blair Hedges of Pennsylvania State University and Richard Thomas of the University of Puerto Rico discovered a tiny lizard that is smaller than any other known lizard. This little reptile, which measures barely more than one-half inch (16 millimeters) long, is a little gecko that lives on the island of Beata in the Dominican Republic. This species is one of more than four dozen new reptiles and amphibians that Hedges and Thomas have discovered in hard-to-reach spots in the Caribbean.

REPRODUCTION

Most female reptiles lay eggs, but some give birth to babies. Some of the newborn babies may have actually hatched from eggs while they were still inside the mother. Female reptiles all lay their eggs or give birth to their babies on land. Even those that live in the water for the rest of the year crawl onto shore to have their young. Tuataras lay eggs in their burrows. Some female turtles and crocodiles bury their eggs on shore or farther inland. A few turtle species lay their eggs in leaf piles. After laying the eggs, a female turtle leaves the nest, and the young are on their own. Crocodiles care for their young, bringing the new hatchlings from the nest site to the water. Snakes and

lizards may lay eggs or have babies. In some species, the female may remain with the eggs and/or the young, although scientists are unsure how much real protection or care many of the mother snakes actually provide.

REPTILES AND PEOPLE

Many people keep reptiles as pets. This can be a problem if the animal bites, if it grows too large, or if it lives too long. Some snakes, for example, can grow to be 6 feet (1.8 meters) long or more, and some turtles can live to be 100 years old. In the wild, most people only see reptiles when the animals are warming themselves in the sun. Usually, the reptile will leave the area as the person draws near. If the animal is surprised, however, some reptiles may bite. Not all snakes are venomous, but some are. A bite from a venomous snake can be dangerous and even deadly and requires an immediate visit to the hospital.

ENDANGERED REPTILES

Reptiles in danger

Many, many species of reptiles may disappear from the Earth soon, if they do not receive some protection. Two-

Reptilian visual displays:
1. Cottonmouth uses gaping mouth as a defensive warning;
2. Frilled lizard looks larger as a defensive display; 3. A ringneck snake draws attention away from its head and shows its coloration as a defense; 4. The alligator snapping turtle uses a food lure to attract its prey;
5. and 6. Territorial or mating displays for green anole (5) and tuatara (6). (Illustration by Dan Erickson. Reproduced by permission.)

thirds of all turtle species, for example, are now listed by the World Conservation Union (IUCN) as being at risk. Overall, the IUCN counts 453 species of reptiles, or more than one in every six species, as being at some risk. Moreover, scientists know so little about many species that others may be at risk, too.

The decline in reptile populations is commonly a result of habitat destruction or of overhunting for their meat or skin or for the pet trade. For turtles, much of the danger comes from the growing number of predator animals that dig up turtle nests and eat the eggs. Scientists estimate, for instance, that 75 to 90

percent of the eggs from some species of North American turtles are lost each year to such predators.

Saving endangered reptiles

In some cases, scientists, government agencies, and/or other concerned groups are protecting the land where the animals live and setting up laws that prevent overhunting. Many zoos are also helping by trying to breed their own captive reptiles. This is especially important for those species that are already very rare.

Too late to save

According to the IUCN, twenty-one species of reptiles are extinct. This includes three snakes, eleven lizards, and seven turtles.

FOR MORE INFORMATION

Books:

Badger, David. *Lizards.* Stillwater, MN: Voyageur Press, 2002.

Behler, John. *Simon and Schuster's Guide to Reptiles and Amphibians of the World.* New York: Simon and Schuster Inc., 1989, 1997.

Cleaver, Andrew. *Snakes and Reptiles: A Portrait of the Animal World.* Wigston, Leicester, England: Magna Books, 1994.

Irwin, Steve, and Terri Irwin. *The Crocodile Hunter.* New York: Penguin Putnam, 1997.

Ivy, Bill. *Nature's Children: Lizards.* Danbury, CT: Grolier, 1990.

Lamar, William. *The World's Most Spectacular Reptiles and Amphibians.* Tampa, FL: World Publications, 1997.

Lockwood, C. C. *The Alligator Book.* Baton Rouge: Louisiana State University Press, 2002.

Mattison, Chris. *Lizards of the World.* New York: Facts on File, 1989.

Mattison, Chris. *The Encyclopedia of Snakes.* New York: DK Publishing Inc., 1997.

McCarthy, Colin. *Eyewitness: Reptile.* New York: DK Publishing, 2000.

Montgomery, Sy. *The Snake Scientist (Scientists in the Field).* Boston, MA: Houghton Mifflin, 2001.

O'Shea, Mark, and Tim Halliday. *Smithsonian Handbooks: Reptiles and Amphibians.* New York: DK Publishing, 2002.

Rue, Leonard Lee. *Alligators and Crocodiles.* Wigston, Leicester, England: Magna Books, 1994.

Tesar, Jenny. *What on Earth is a Tuatara?* Woodbridge, CT: Blackbirch Press, 1994.

Periodicals:

Barr, Brady, and Margaret Zackowitz. "The Big Squeeze. (The Icky Adventure of Brady Barr)." *National Geographic Kids.* May 2003, page 40.

Calvert, Pam. "Out of Control!: The Brown Tree Snake." *Odyssey.* April 2000, page 23.

Chiang, Mona. "The Plight of the Turtle." *Science World.* May 9, 2003, page 8.

Gill, Paul G., Jr. "Red on Yellow, Kill a Fellow! Get Snake-smart before Heading into the Wild." *Boys' Life.* April 2004, page 26.

Mealy, Nora Steiner. "Creatures from Komodo." *Ranger Rick.* August 2001, page 18.

Murphy, Thomas J. "Swamp Wars." *Boys' Life.* November 2000, page 10.

Myers, Jack. "Flicking tongues." *Highlights for Children.* September 1997, page 32.

O'Meara, Stephen. "Creature from the Black Lagoon." *Odyssey.* March 1999, page 42.

Scheid, Darrin. "It's a Bird! It's a Plane! It's a Snake." *Boys' Life.* January 2003, page 11.

Swarts, Candice. "The Tortoise and the Pair." *National Geographic Kids.* October 2003, page 14.

Thompson, Sharon. "Attention, Lizard Parents." *National Geographic World.* May 2002, page 6.

Web sites:

"All About Turtles." Gulf of Maine Aquarium. http://octopus .gma.org/turtles/ (accessed on November 1, 2004).

"How fast can a crocodile run?" Crocodilian Biology Database, Florida Museum of Natural History. http://www.flmnh.ufl .edu/natsci/herpetology/brittoncrocs/cbd-faq-q4.htm (accessed on November 1, 2004).

"Reptiles." Environmental Education for Kids. http://www.dnr .state.wi.us/org/caer/ce/eek/critter/reptile/index.htm (accessed on November 1, 2004).

"Reptiles." San Diego Natural History Museum. http://www.sdnhm .org/exhibits/reptiles/index.html (accessed on November 1, 2004).

"Snakes." Defenders of Wildlife. http://www.kidsplanet.org/ factsheets/snakes.html (accessed on November 1, 2004).

Sohn, Emily. "The Cool Side of Snake Pits." *Science News for Kids.* http://www.sciencenewsforkids.org/articles/20030625/ Note2.asp (accessed on November 1, 2004).

Sohn, Emily. "Delivering a Little Snake Venom." *Science News for Kids.* http://www.sciencenewsforkids.org/articles/20030903/ Feature1.asp (accessed on November 1, 2004).

Trivedi, Bigal P. "Smallest Known Lizard Found in Caribbean." *National Geographic.* http://news.nationalgeographic.com/ news/2001/12/1203_TVtinylizard.html (accessed on November 1, 2004).

NIGHT LIZARDS
Xantusiidae

Class: Reptilia

Order: Squamata

Suborder: Scincomorpha

Family: Xantusiidae

Number of species: 23 species

PHYSICAL CHARACTERISTICS

The night lizards are mainly small lizards without the working eyelids that many other species of lizards have. Instead, the night lizards have a see-through scale covering the eye. This clear scale, which looks somewhat similar to a person's contact lens, is called a spectacle. Beneath the spectacle, the eyes of some species of night lizards have catlike pupils, but others have round pupils. The typical night lizard has a low flat body, which allows it to sneak easily into cracks of rocks or into narrow openings between plant leaves.

The bodies of these lizards are covered with small scales, except on the head and belly. The top of the head is covered with large plates, and wide rectangular scales stretch across the belly. Most have drab-colored bodies, usually brown or gray, but a few have striking patterns. The granite night lizard, for example, has a spotted leopard-style pattern of brown spots on an otherwise yellowish body. Some have round and bumpy scales that give the lizard's back the look of a tiny beaded purse. Some night lizards are quite small, reaching only 1.5 inches (3.7 centimeters) long from the tip of the snout to the vent, a slit-like opening at the beginning of the tail and on the underside of the lizard. Adults of the largest species, the yellow-spotted night lizard, grow to more than three times that size, reaching 5 inches (12.7 centimeters) long from the snout to the vent. The typical night lizard has a tail as long or slightly longer than its body.

GEOGRAPHIC RANGE

Night lizards live in the United States, Cuba, and Mexico, as well as in Central America as far south as Panama.

phylum

class

subclass

order

monotypic order

suborder

▲ **family**

HABITAT

Each night lizard species is very picky about where it makes its home. Some species live only in very dry areas, like rocky deserts. Others only live in the rotting parts of certain types of plants or in the dead leaves or decaying logs laying on the ground in a rainforest. Some night lizards even prefer life in a cave. Although members of the family live in North America, Central America, and Cuba, they stay in small areas within that range. For example, the only part of the United States that is home to night lizards is the Southwest, and the Cuban night lizard makes its home in a tiny part of Cuba, where it lives under rocks or buried in soil in areas of dry warm forest.

DIET

Many night lizards, like the Cuban night lizard, eat insects and spiders. The yellow-spotted night lizard also eats scorpions and other invertebrates (in-VER-teh-brehts), which are animals without backbones. Others, such as the island night lizard, eat at least some seeds and other bits of plants. Scientists are unsure if any species are strict vegetarians that eat only plants. Species in this family search for food where they live. For example, a yellow-spotted night lizard that lives in rotting logs usually looks there for its next meal.

BEHAVIOR AND REPRODUCTION

People rarely see night lizards during the daytime, but they actually can be active both night and day, if the daytime temperatures are not too hot. Even on the best of days, however, they spend most of their time out of sight under dead leaves, inside plants, or in the cracks of rocks. They are much more likely to venture outside at night, when they may scramble about under the cover of darkness. Scientists still know very little about the behavior of night lizards.

Females of all night lizard species, except one, give birth to baby lizards. The typical litter holds five to eight babies. The

Cuban night lizard is the only species in this family that lays eggs. The female lays a single egg at a time, dropping it into a hole. The egg hatches two months later.

In most lizard species, a female becomes pregnant only after she mates with a male. Some night lizards do not follow this rule, and the females can become pregnant on their own. Among female yellow-spotted night lizards, some mate with males to become pregnant, but others may not even see males. Some groups of yellow-spotted night lizards that live in Costa Rica and Panama are made up of only females. With no males in sight, the females are able to become pregnant themselves and have perfectly healthy babies.

NIGHT LIZARDS AND PEOPLE

Although some people believe they are venomous, night lizards are not. They are harmless to humans.

CONSERVATION STATUS

According to the World Conservation Union (IUCN), one species of night lizard is Vulnerable, which means that it faces a high risk of extinction in the wild. The U.S. Fish and Wildlife Service lists the same species, the island night lizard, as Threatened, which means that it is likely to become endangered in the foreseeable future. The island night lizard is at risk because people have brought pigs and goats to the three small Channel Islands where the lizard lives. These much larger animals eat the plants that the lizards use as their homes. Efforts are now under way to remove pigs and goats from at least one of the three islands. Although no other species have been named as being at risk, many night lizards are threatened by habitat destruction. When humans cut down rainforests, remove plants, or otherwise destroy the places where the lizards live, whole populations of these animals can disappear.

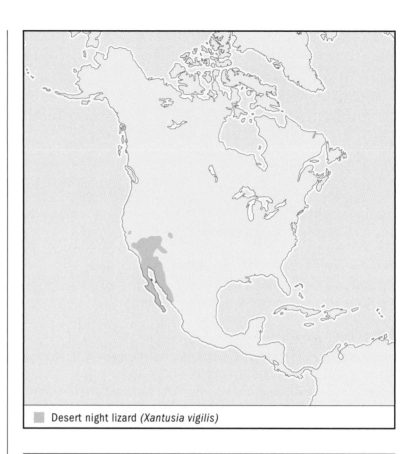

Desert night lizard (*Xantusia vigilis*)

DESERT NIGHT LIZARD
Xantusia vigilis

Physical characteristics: Among the smallest species in this family, the desert night lizards grow to only 1.5 inches (3.7 centimeters) long from the tip of the snout to the vent. Like other night lizards, they have no working eyelids. This lizard usually has dark spots on its brown back, although in some areas, the back may have a green, yellow, or orange tint. Its skin is typically wrinkly on the neck and along the sides of the body.

Geographic range: This species makes its home in small areas within the southwestern United States and northwestern Mexico.

Habitat: The desert night lizard also goes by the common name yucca night lizard, because it spends much of its time in clumps of

rotting yucca (YUCK-uh) plants. It also lives in old, dead agave (uh-GA-vee) plants.

Diet: The desert night lizard eats ants and beetles and occasionally some other insects that it finds in the plants where it lives.

Behavior and reproduction: This lizard likes to stay hidden in yucca or agave plants. Males and females mate in late spring, and about three months later, the females have their young. The typical brood includes one to three baby lizards. Sometimes, if the weather is especially dry, females may skip a year between births.

Desert night lizards and people: Although desert night lizards can be very numerous in some places, with twelve thousand individuals in an area of just one square mile (or four thousand in a square-kilometer area), people rarely see this shy lizard. Humans can, however, harm the lizard populations by cutting down and removing yucca and agave plants, which often happens when they clear land to make way for houses.

Conservation status: This species is not considered endangered or threatened. ■

FOR MORE INFORMATION

Books:

Alvarez del Toro, M. *Los reptiles de Chiapas.* 3rd edition. Chiapas, Mexico: Instituto de Historia Natural, Tuxtla Gutierrez, 1982.

Behler, John, and F. Wayne King. "Night Lizards Family (Xantusidae)" *National Audubon Society Field Guide to Reptiles and Amphibians.* New York: Alfred A. Knopf, 1979.

Campbell, J. A. *Amphibians and Reptiles of Northern Guatemala, the Yucatan, and Belize.* Norman: University of Oklahoma Press, 1998.

Estes, R. *Sauria terrestria, Amphisbaenia.* Vol. 10A, *Handbuch der Palaeoherpetologie.* Stuttgart: Gustav Fisher Verlag, 1983.

Halliday, Tim, and Kraig Adler. *The Encyclopedia of Reptiles and Amphibians.* New York: Facts on File, 1986.

Mattison, Chris. *Lizards of the World.* New York: Facts on File, 1989.

Mautz, W. J. "Ecology and Energetics of the Island Night Lizard, *Xantusia riversiana,* on San Clemente Island." In *Third California Islands Symposium: Recent Advances in Research on the California Islands,* edited by F. G. Hochberg. Santa Barbara: Santa Barbara Museum of Natural History, 1993.

Web sites:

"Family Xantusiidae (Night Lizards)." Animal Diversity Web. University of Michigan Museum of Zoology. http://animaldiversity.ummz.umich.edu/ site/accounts/classification/Xantusiidae.html (accessed on November 15, 2004).

"Granite Night Lizard." Western Ecological Research Center, U.S. Geological Survey Biological Resources Division. http://www.werc.usgs .gov/fieldguide/xahe.htm (accessed on November 15, 2004).

"Island Night Lizard." eNature. http://www.enature.com/fieldguide/ showSpeciesSH.asp?curGroupID=7&shapeID=1059&curPageNum= 50&recnum=AR0662 (accessed on November 16, 2004).

"Night Lizard." Wikipedia, the free encyclopedia. http://en.wikipedia.org/ wiki/Xantusiidae (accessed on November 15, 2004).

WALL LIZARDS, ROCK LIZARDS, AND RELATIVES

Lacertidae

Class: Reptilia

Order: Squamata

Suborder: Sauria

Family: Lacertidae

Number of species: at least 225 species

phylum

class

subclass

order

monotypic order

suborder

▲ **family**

PHYSICAL CHARACTERISTICS

The wall and rock lizards, and their relatives, are small to medium-sized lizards with strong legs, especially the larger back pair, and usually very long tails. The typical wall or rock lizard has small beaded scales on its back and large square or rectangular scales on its belly. They come in many different colors and patterns from an almost entirely green or drab brown body to a bluish body with black blotches, a body split into a red front and black-and-white speckled back, or a black and cream striped body and red legs. Some species have brightly colored tails, which attract the attention of predators (PREH-duh-ters), or animals that hunt them for food. Fortunately, the lizards can easily drop their tails if they are attacked, allowing the lizard, minus its tail, to escape. In many species, the males have more spectacular colors than the females, and males in some species become even more brilliantly hued during the mating season.

The average adult grows to less than 8 inches (20 centimeters) long from head to tail, although a few species in this large family can reach 20 inches (50 centimeters) in length. Of their total length, much can be tail. In some species, such as the oriental six-lined runner, three-quarters of their overall length is tail.

GEOGRAPHIC RANGE

Wall and rock lizards live in Europe, Asia, Africa, and the East Indies.

HABITAT

Wall and rock lizards are very common in dry areas, such as deserts, but some species make their homes in forests or in very cold areas, such as grasslands high up in the mountains or in far northern lands inside the Arctic Circle. They are also found on some Atlantic Ocean islands, including the Canaries off northern Africa, Sri Lanka (or Ceylon) off the southern tip of India, and the British Isles.

DIET

The bellies of these lizards are usually filled with insects, which they typically capture by sitting very still in one spot—usually in the shade—until an insect wanders by. They then spring out and grab the tasty morsel. This type of hunting is called ambush. The western sandveld lizard is unusual because while it eats some insects, its main diet is scorpions, which the lizard finds by looking for their tunnel entrances and digging them out of the ground. Some species in this lizard family also eat seeds and fruit in addition to insects. A few, including the adult giant lizards that live in the Canary Islands, are unique in that they eat almost only plant material.

BEHAVIOR AND REPRODUCTION

Active during the day, wall and rock lizards typically like to sunbathe, or bask, to warm up their bodies. Most of them bask out in the open on rocks or on the ground. Some, such as Asian grass lizards, climb into plants and bushes and use their very long tails to wrap around stalks and branches. A few species, like the western sandveld lizard, stay in underground burrows most of the time.

Usually the lizards are able to avoid predators by keeping careful watch and running for cover before an attacker can come too close. The shovel-snouted lizard is even able to dive into the sand of its desert home and bury itself. This lizard scoots even deeper when it wants to take a cool and safe nap. Young Kalahari sand lizards have another defensive tactic. These baby lizards look so much like a bad-tasting beetle, known as the oogpister, that predators avoid them. Despite these behaviors, however, attackers are sometimes able to approach wall and rock lizards closely enough to attack them. When this happens, a wall or rock lizard can drop its tail, leaving the tail for the predator while the lizard escapes. A replacement tail grows, but it is usually much shorter.

Almost all the lizards in this family lay eggs and usually fewer than ten at a time. A female digs a hole in the ground and lays her eggs there. In many cases, the mother digs the nest under a rock that is out in the open and can warm up in the sun. The underground soil keeps the soft-shelled eggs moist. She then leaves the nest; the eggs hatch later, and the young are on their own. The largest females lay the most eggs, with some female eyed lizards giving birth to twenty eggs at a time. The females of a few members of this family have baby lizards rather than eggs. This includes the viviparous (vie-VIH-puh-rus) lizard, which lives in northern Europe. Females of this species mate with the males in the spring to early summer and have four to eleven babies three or four months later. Seven species in this family are all females, but they can still have babies, which are also all females.

WALL LIZARDS, ROCK LIZARDS, THEIR RELATIVES, AND PEOPLE

People usually leave these lizards alone, but long ago, some humans hunted and ate the giant lizards of the Canary Islands.

A LOSING TAIL

Many lizards, including the wall and rock lizards of the family Lacertidae, can drop their tails when they are attacked. The dropped tail wiggles around on the ground and draws the attention of the attacker while the lizard runs for its life. Wall and rock lizards can drop their tails because their tails are made of a series of small bones that have weak points between them. The lizard also has a ring of strong muscles around each weak point. When attacked, the lizard squeezes the ring of muscles so tightly that the weak point in the tail snaps and the tail falls off. After it drops, nerves in the tail continue to work sometimes for many minutes, and the tail busily squirms along the ground. Eventually, the tail stops moving, but by then, the lizard is long gone.

CONSERVATION STATUS

According to the World Conservation Union (IUCN), Simony's giant lizard is Critically Endangered, which means that it faces an extremely high risk of extinction in the wild. This giant lizard is so rare that scientists actually thought it was extinct until a small population turned up in 1975 high in the cliffs of El Hierro, one of the Canary Islands. Another species, called the Gomeran giant lizard, was similarly thought to be extinct until 2001 when a population was discovered in the Canaries. It may be even more rare than Simony's giant lizard, but the IUCN has not yet listed it as being at risk. The greatest predators to these lizards are cats and rats, which were both brought to the islands by humans.

In addition to Simony's giant lizard and the Gomeran giant lizard, the IUCN has listed Clark's lacerta as Endangered, which means that it faces a very high risk of extinction in the wild, and five others as Vulnerable, which means that they run a high risk of extinction in the wild. The U.S. Fish and Wildlife Service lists the Hierro giant lizard as Endangered, or in danger of extinction throughout all or a significant portion of its range, and the Ibiza wall lizard as Threatened, or likely to become endangered in the foreseeable future.

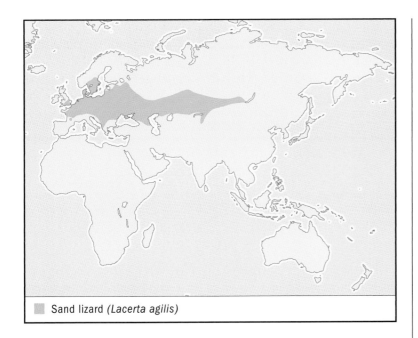

Sand lizard (*Lacerta agilis*)

SAND LIZARD
Lacerta agilis

Physical characteristics: One of the larger members of this family, the biggest sand lizards can grow to almost 12 inches (30 centimeters) long from the tip of the head to the end of their long tail. Most, however, reach only about 8 inches (20 centimeters) long. In the eastern part of its range, the sand lizards may be greenish, but western lizards are usually brown or gray with dark spots and/or stripes. Males of the western sand lizards also show some green along their sides and on their bellies and become brighter green during the mating season.

Geographic range: The sand lizard lives in spotty areas throughout Europe and Asia, from the British Isles to China, and as far south as Greece.

Habitat: The sand lizard is common in places with sandy soils, such as sand dunes and brushy areas, but it can also make its home in clay-type soils along forest edges and in fields and gardens.

Diet: It lives mostly on insects, which it hunts by looking for them while skittering through cover in its habitat. It will also sometimes

eat worms and other invertebrates (in-VER-teh-brehts), which are animals without backbones, as well as fruit and flowers, and once in a while even another sand lizard.

Behavior and reproduction: The sand lizard is active during the day and will run through brush above ground or bask in warm spots, but it usually stays out of sight. This shy lizard often darts into holes or tunnels it finds among plant roots when it feels the least bit threatened. Numerous sand lizards may live together in the same area. In colder climates, they will hibernate from fall to early spring.

During the breeding season in the spring, the males turn into fighters and will battle one another over the chance to mate with a female. The fights usually involve the males grasping each other's necks, and then wrestling until one gives up and leaves. After mating with a male, a female finds a sunny spot where she digs a hole and lays three to fourteen eggs. She provides no care for the eggs or her young. In forty to sixty days, the eggs hatch.

Sand lizards and people: Humans and this lizard rarely see one another.

Conservation status: Although neither the IUCN nor the U.S. Fish and Wildlife Service list this species as threatened, some populations are at great risk because of the destruction of their habitat. In western Europe, the lizards typically live in heathlands, which are open areas covered with low plants and shrubs. When the heathlands are destroyed to make way for homes or other human development, the lizards disappear. ■

FOR MORE INFORMATION

Books:

Behler, John, and F. Wayne King. "Typical Old World Lizard Family (Lacertidae)," *National Audubon Society Field Guide to Reptiles and Amphibians.* New York: Alfred A. Knopf, 1979.

Böhme, W., ed. *Handbuch der Reptilien und Amphibien Europas.* 2 vols. Wiesbaden, Germany: AULA Verlag, 1984–1986.

Branch, B. *Field Guide to the Snakes and Other Reptiles of Southern Africa.* Capetown, South Africa: Struik Publishers, 1998.

Burnie, David, and Don Wilson, eds. *The Definitive Visual Guide to the World's Wildlife* New York: DK Publishing, 2001.

Halliday, Tim, and Kraig Adler. *The Encyclopedia of Reptiles and Amphibians.* New York: Facts on File, 1986.

Mattison, Chris. *Lizards of the World.* New York: Facts on File, 1989.

Valakos, E.D., W. Böhme, V. Perez-Mellado, and P. Maragou, eds. *Lacertids of the Mediterranean Region: A Biological Approach.* Athens, Greece: Hellenic Zoological Society, 1993.

Web sites:

"Common lizard, viviparous lizard." BBC. http://www.bbc.co.uk/nature/wildfacts/factfiles/282.shtml (accessed on November 19, 2004).

"*Lacerta agilis*—Sand Lizard." First Nature. http://www.first-nature.com/reptiles/lacerta_vivipara.htm (accessed on November 19, 2004).

"*Lacerta vivipara*—Common Lizard." First Nature. http://www.first-nature.com/reptiles/lacerta_agilis.htm (accessed on November 19, 2004).

"Sand Lizard." BBC. http://www.bbc.co.uk/nature/wildfacts/factfiles/283.shtml (accessed on November 19, 2004).

"Sand Lizard (*Lacerta agilis*)." ARKive. http://www.arkive.org/species/ARK/reptiles/Lacerta_agilis/more_moving_images.html (accessed on November 19, 2004).

MICROTEIIDS
Gymnophthalmidae

Class: Reptilia

Order: Squamata

Suborder: Lacertiformes

Family: Gymnophthalmidae

Number of species: At least 175 species

PHYSICAL CHARACTERISTICS

The microteiids are very small lizards, with adults usually only growing to 2.3 inches (6 centimeters) long from the tip of the snout to the vent, which is a slitlike opening between the two hind legs on the underside of the lizard. Their tails come in different lengths depending on the species, but they are typically about one and one-half times the length of the body from snout to vent or longer. All species in this family can easily break off the tail and grow a new one. Most, but not all, have four working legs. The eighteen species in the group, or genus (GEE-nus), called *Bachia* have tiny legs, and those in the genus *Calyptommatus* have no legs at all. A genus is a group of similar species. Although the microteiids spend much of their time hidden in dark places, they have well-formed eyes.

Many species in this family have small scales on their backs and larger scales on their undersides. Some species have ridges, or keels, on their back scales, and some have smooth unkeeled scales. Many have backs in shades of brown or black, and some have stripes or spots. In a few species, such as the golden spectacled lizard of Costa Rica, the tail may be a different color than the rest of the lizard.

GEOGRAPHIC RANGE

Microteiids live in southern Mexico, in Central America, on the Caribbean islands, and throughout much of South America, where they reach as far south as north-central Argentina.

HABITAT

The microteiids live in tropical forests, often by water. They usually stay out of sight under piles of leaves, beneath logs, or in other hiding places and will often dive into the water to escape predators (PREH-duh-ters), or animals that hunt other animals for food.

DIET

These lizards are mainly active during the day and spend much of their time rooting around in leaves and along the ground to find their favorite food insects. They see and smell well and likely use these characteristics to help them find food and to escape predators.

BEHAVIOR AND REPRODUCTION

Although this family has at least 175 species, their small size and tendency to remain hidden has helped to keep much of their behavior a secret from scientists. Some have, however, been seen wandering along the forest floor and along the shores of streams and swamps looking for insects to eat. When they feel threatened by an attacker, they will run to the water, where they dive in and swim off. Many have flattened tails, which help them swim quickly through the water. Unlike most other lizards, which sunbathe, or bask, out in the open during the day to warm their bodies, the microteiid lizards apparently do not. Instead, some appear to heat up their bodies by finding a sunny spot and crawling under leaves there.

Those species that have been studied are all egg layers, and scientists believe that the females only have one or two young at a time but lay eggs more than once a year. Some of the species are all female, which means that they can and do have babies without mating with males. Species that do this are called parthenogenic (PAR-thih-no-JEH-nik). This is rather unusual among lizards and among other vertebrates (VER-teh-brehts),

WHAT GOOD ARE THEY?

Scientists do not understand just how important each individual species is to life on Earth. Over the years, the most-studied animals are those that humans find cute and/or want for pets, like dogs and cats; that people find useful, like cows for meat and horses for farm chores; or bothersome, like mosquitoes that transmit disease. Scientists know much less about other species that lack these traits and that stay out of sight. The microteiid lizards are an example. They are small lizards that hide in piles of leaves and rarely come across a person. Even these species, however, are important to the web of life on the planet. For example, numerous predator species probably eat them, and they in turn eat many different types of insects, which eat other animals and plants, and so on. If the microteiid lizards were to disappear, it is possible that the surrounding environment would change so much that it would cause harm to the other animals and plants that live there. This is also true of other species on Earth. No animal or plant lives and dies without having an effect on some other living thing.

which are mammals, birds, and other animals with backbones. Most vertebrates require that a female and male mate before the female becomes pregnant. In the microteiid lizards, however, a female can become pregnant without ever seeing a male and produces babies that are her exact duplicates. Such exact duplicates are called clones.

MICROTEIIDS AND PEOPLE

People and microteiid lizards rarely come across one another. Sometimes, however, people unknowingly dig in their habitat and can harm the lizards.

CONSERVATION STATUS

These species are not considered endangered or threatened, but scientists know little about them. Because they live along the ground, however, and sometimes in very small areas, habitat destruction can wipe out entire populations.

Bachia bresslaui

NO COMMON NAME
Bachia bresslaui

Physical characteristics: This lizard is known only by its scientific name of *Bachia bresslaui*. It has a long body and long tail but very tiny, hardly noticeable legs. Its upper body is gray to brown, sometimes with brown spots, and has a tan stripe down either side. It has a cream-colored underside. Unlike many other lizards that have noticeable

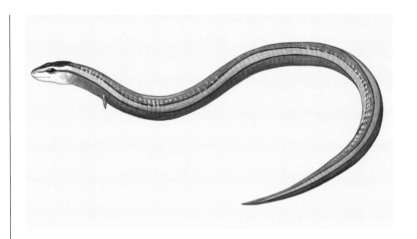

Bachia bresslaui *live in the South American countries of Paraguay and Brazil. (Illustration by Barbara Duperron. Reproduced by permission.)*

openings on the sides of the head for ears, this species has no such openings. Of the few individuals that have ever been seen, the largest of this rare species of lizards reached a size of 4.2 inches (10.6 centimeters) in length from the snout to the vent, plus a tail that measured more than 6.3 inches (16 centimeters) long.

Geographic range: They live in the South American countries of Paraguay and Brazil.

Habitat: In their range, which includes the northeastern area of Paraguay and central Brazil, these lizards have been found beneath pastures inside tunnels in sandy soils. Scientists think they may live in other types of soil, too.

Diet: Scientists have studied only five individuals from this species. These five ate ants, scorpions, spiders, beetles, and beetle grubs.

Behavior and reproduction: Although very little is known about *Bachia bresslaui*, scientists believe these lizards likely leave their below-earth homes and search about above ground for insects and other things to eat. They may walk with their small legs or slither like snakes. Scientists also guess that the females lay eggs rather than have baby lizards, but they have not yet found the eggs. They are also unsure about how many eggs the lizards lay at a time.

***Bachia bresslaui* and people:** People and this lizard rarely see one another. Humans do, however, sometimes destroy their habitat when they build on or otherwise change the areas where the lizards live.

Conservation status: This species is not considered endangered or threatened. Scientists suspect that this species may actually live in areas other than northeastern Paraguay and central Brazil, but they do not have proof as yet. ■

FOR MORE INFORMATION

Books:

Avila-Pires, T. C. S. *Lizards of Brazilian Amazonia (Reptilia: Squamata).* Leiden, Germany: Zoologische Verhandelingen, 1995.

Cogger, H. G., and R. G. Zweifel, eds. *Encyclopedia of Reptiles and Amphibians.* 2nd ed. San Diego: Academic Press, 1998.

Dixon, J. R., and P. Soini. *The Reptiles of the Upper Amazon River Basin, Iquitos Region, Peru.* 2nd rev. ed. Milwaukee: Milwaukee Public Museum, 1986.

Mattison, Chris. *Lizards of the World.* New York, NY: Facts on File, 1989.

Murphy, J. C. *Amphibians and Reptiles of Trinidad and Tobago.* Malabar, FL: Krieger, 1997.

Pianka, E. R., and L. J. Vitt. *Lizards: Windows to the Evolution of Diversity.* Berkeley: University of California Press, 2003.

Pough, F. H., R. M. Andrews, J. E. Cadle, M. L. Crump, A. H. Savitzky, and K. D. Wells. *Herpetology.* 2nd ed. Upper Saddle River, NJ: Prentice Hall, 2001.

Powell, R., and R. W. Henderson, eds. *Contributions to West Indian Herpetology: A Tribute to Albert Schwartz.* Contributions to Herpetology, Volume 12. Ithaca, NY: Society for the Study of Amphibians and Reptiles, 1996.

Schwartz, A., and R. W. Henderson. *Amphibians and Reptiles of the West Indies: Descriptions, Distributions, and Natural History.* Gainesville, FL: University of Florida Press, 1991.

Vitt, L. J., and S. de la Torre. *A Research Guide to the Lizards of Cuyabeno.* Museo de Zoologia (QCAZ) Centro de Biodiversidad y Ambiente Pontificia Universidad Catolica del Ecuador, 1996.

Zug, G. R., L. J. Vitt, and J. L. Caldwell. *Herpetology: An Introductory Biology of Amphibians and Reptiles.* 2nd ed. San Diego: Academic Press, 2001.

Web sites:

"A Brief Look at the Gymnophthalmidae Spectacled Lizards and Microteiids." Cyberlizard. http://www.nafcon.dircon.co.uk/gymnophthalmidae. htm (accessed on November 12, 2004).

"Genus *Bachia.*" Animal Diversity Web. University of Michigan Museum of Zoology. http://animaldiversity.ummz.umich.edu/site/accounts/classification/Bachia.html (accessed on November 15, 2004).

burrows. Many make their own burrows, but some move into other animals' burrows instead. A few species live near streams and wetlands and often go for a swim. The Paraguayan caiman lizard, for instance, is an excellent swimmer that glides through the water with its powerful tail.

DIET

Most of the whiptails, tegus, and other members of this family will eat nearly any type of insect they find, and some large species will also eat fruit. The tegus eat fruit, too, but will also eat eggs, as well as living or dead animals. The Caiman lizards eat mostly snails, which they find while swimming in streams and swamps. Larger species, such as the giant ameivas that grow to be about 2 feet (61 centimeters) long, will eat small vertebrates (VER-teh-brehts), which are animals with backbones. They will also eat fruit that has fallen to the ground from plants and trees.

The lizards in this family usually hunt for their food with their keen eyesight or with their good sense of smell. Some species can pick up odors especially well and can even find insects that are buried underground.

BEHAVIOR AND REPRODUCTION

The majority of these species spend their nights in burrows, then crawl out on sunny mornings to bask. Once they are warm, they begin running here and there looking for things to eat. When they get too hot, they find some shade, and when they start to get cold, they soak up the rays in a sunny spot. Often, many individuals will live in the same area, and they usually get along very well. When breeding season starts, however, the males will fight over the females.

All of the females lay eggs, rather than giving birth to babies. Some species lay only one or two eggs, while others lay thirty or more. The largest species have the most eggs, and the smallest species, the least. In addition, the larger older females usually lay more eggs than smaller younger females of the same species. For instance, a female six-lined racerunner may lay only one or two eggs her first year but three or four her second year. Most females lay their eggs in underground burrows, rotting logs, leaf piles, or some other slightly moist place. Some species drag leaves and other plant bits into their burrows and build nests for the eggs. The females stay with their eggs until they hatch.

Some species in this family are all female—they have no males and do not need them to have babies. The females give birth to young that are clones, which are perfect copies, of themselves.

WHIPTAIL LIZARDS, TEGUS, THEIR RELATIVES, AND PEOPLE

Some people hunt these lizards for their meat, fat, and/or skin, and others capture them for the pet trade.

CONSERVATION STATUS

According to the World Conservation Union (IUCN), two species are Extinct, which means they are no longer in existence. In addition, two are Critically Endangered and face an extremely high risk of extinction in the wild, and one is Vulnerable and faces a high risk of extinction in the wild. The IUCN also describes two species as Data Deficient, which means that scientists do not have enough information to make a judgment about the threat of extinction. The U.S. Fish and Wildlife Service also lists two species as Threatened or likely to become endangered in the foreseeable future. Many of the at-risk species naturally have low numbers because they only live on small islands. In this case, habitat destruction and/or collection can wipe out whole populations and possibly entire species.

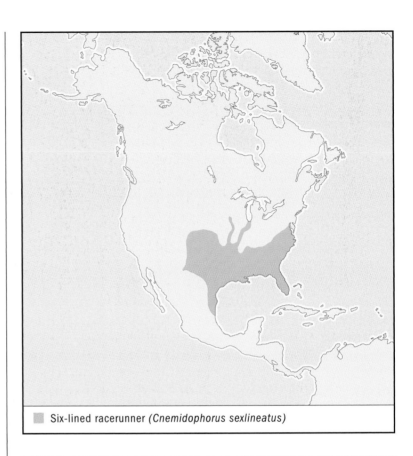

Six-lined racerunner *(Cnemidophorus sexlineatus)*

SIX-LINED RACERUNNER
Cnemidophorus sexlineatus

Physical characteristics: The six-lined racerunner is a handsome and speedy little lizard. Its body is brown to green and has six thin yellow stripes that flow down the body from head to tail. Each stripe is separated from the next with a wide brown to black band of color. In addition, a lighter brown to gray stripe runs down the center of its back. In some populations, the head and neck are brownish, but in others they are yellowish green. Juveniles have blue or blue-green tails. Adults reach about 2.1 to 2.9 inches (5.5 to 7.5 centimeters) in length from their snout to the vent. Including the tail, they can grow to 3.3 inches (8.5 centimeters) in length. Females are usually a bit larger than males.

Geographic range: This lizard lives mainly in the southeastern quarter of the United States but also in a few areas of northern midwestern states.

Habitat: This lizard commonly makes its home in sandy areas that have lots of sun but also some shady spots where it can cool off or hide from predators (PREH-duh-ters), or animals that hunt it for food.

Diet: They eat a variety of insects, spiders, and land snails.

Behavior and reproduction: After spending the night in their burrows, these lizards come out in the morning after the sun has warmed the ground. They bask to heat up their bodies and then spend much of the rest of the day looking for food. They are extremely fast lizards for their size and quickly dart into burrows, clumps of grass, shrubby undergrowth, or some other hiding spot when they feel even slightly threatened. They can run almost 18 miles (28 kilometers) an hour. During the breeding season, the chin and chest in some males (those from the western part of the species' range) turn a bluish white, while the females' undersides remain all white. They mate in spring to early summer. Females usually lay one to six eggs, which hatch in early to mid-summer. Some females have a second clutch, or batch of eggs, later in the year. They provide no care for the eggs or the young.

Six-lined racerunners and people: Other than occasionally collecting one for a pet, people generally leave this lizard alone.

Conservation status: This species is not considered endangered or threatened.   ■

Crocodile tegu (*Crocodilurus lacertinus*)

CROCODILE TEGU
Crocodilurus lacertinus

Physical characteristics: The tail of a crocodile tegu is very long and stretches twice as long as the rest of its body. It also has pointy scales that stand up in a row like those on a crocodile's tail. Adults are mostly greenish brown or brown with a whitish or yellow underside. Their legs have some orange spots. Adults grow to about 19.7 inches (50 centimeters) in length from head to tail.

Geographic range: They are found in South America in the area surrounding the Amazon and Orinoco rivers.

With its crocodilelike tail, the crocodile tegu is an excellent swimmer. (©Jany Sauvanet/ Photo Researchers, Inc. Reproduced by permission.)

Habitat: Crocodile tegus wander in the woods and swim in streams.

Diet: They eat almost any insect or spider they can find on land or in the water.

Behavior and reproduction: With its crocodilelike tail, the crocodile tegu is an excellent swimmer. Females lay eggs. Scientists know little about its other behaviors or its reproduction.

Crocodile tegus and people: Humans and crocodile tegus rarely see or bother one another in the wild.

Conservation status: This species is not considered endangered or threatened. ■

FOR MORE INFORMATION

Books

Badger, D. *Lizards: A Natural History of Some Uncommon Creatures— Extraordinary Chameleons, Iguanas, Geckos, and More.* Stillwater, MN: Voyageur Press, 2002.

Cogger, H. G., and R. G. Zweifel, eds. *Reptiles and Amphibians.* New York: Smithmark, 1992.

Degenhardt, W. G., C. W. Painter, and A. H. Price. *Amphibians and Reptiles of New Mexico.* Albuquerque: University of New Mexico Press, 1996.

Fitzgerald, L. A., J. M. Chani, and O. E. Donadio. "*Tupinambis* Lizards in Argentina: Implementing Management of a Traditionally Exploited Resource." In *Neotropical Wildlife Use and Conservation*, edited by J. G. Robinson and K. H. Redford. Chicago: University of Chicago Press, 1996.

Harding, J., and J. Holman. *Michigan Turtles and Lizards.* Lansing: Michigan State University Museum, 1990.

Lamar, W. *The World's Most Spectacular Reptiles and Amphibians.* Tampa, FL: World Publications, 1997.

Mattison, Chris. *Lizards of the World.* New York, NY: Facts on File, 1989.

Palmer, W. M., and A. L. Braswell. *Reptiles of North Carolina.* Chapel Hill: University of North Carolina Press, 1995.

Pianka, E. R., and L. J. Vitt. *Lizards: Windows to the Evolution of Diversity.* Berkeley: University of California Press, 2003.

Pough, F. H., R. M. Andrews, J. E. Cadle, M. L. Crump, A. H. Savitzky, and K. D. Wells. *Herpetology.* 2nd ed. Upper Saddle River, NJ: Prentice Hall, 2001.

Wright, J. W., and L. J. Vitt. *Biology of Whiptail Lizards, Genus Cnemidophorus.* Norman: Oklahoma Museum of Natural History, 1993.

Web sites

"Great Basin Whiptail." California Living Museum. http://www.calmzoo .org/stories/storyReader$81 (accessed on November 5, 2004).

"Lizards of Wisconsin: Special Tricks." Environmental Education for Kids, Wisconsin Department of Natural Resources. http://dnr.wi.gov/org/ caer/ce/eek/critter/reptile/lizardsOfWisconsin5.htm (accessed on November 5, 2004).

McFarlane, B. "*Cnemidophorus sexlineatus.*" Animal Diversity Web, University of Michigan Museum of Zoology. http://animaldiversity.ummz .umich.edu/site/accounts/information/Cnemidophorus_sexlineatus .html (accessed on November 5, 2004).

"Prairie Racerunner." Environmental Education for Kids, Wisconsin Department of Natural Resources. http://www.dnr.state.wi.us/org/ caer/ce/eek/critter/reptile/prairieracerunner.htm (accessed on November 5, 2004).

"Six-Lined Racerunner." Davidson College Biology Department. http://www.bio.davidson.edu/Biology/herpcons/Herps_of_NC/lizards/ Cne_sex.html (accessed on November 5, 2004).

"Unisexual Whiptail Lizards." American Museum of Natural History. http://www.amnh.org/exhibitions/expeditions/treasure_fossil/Treasures/ Unisexual_Whiptail_Lizards/lizards.html?50 (accessed on November 5, 2004).

**GIRDLED AND PLATED
LIZARDS**

Cordylidae

Class: Reptilia

Order: Squamata

Suborder: Sauria

Family: Cordylidae

Number of species: 88 species

PHYSICAL CHARACTERISTICS

The plated lizards and the girdled lizards, which have often been separated into their own individual families, are heavy-bodied lizards. The plated lizards have tails that are much longer than the body and are covered with long, rectangular scales. Girdled lizards include the flat lizards, girdle-tailed lizards, and the grass and snake lizards. They have shorter tails that are only about the same length as the rest of the body and are usually covered with spiny scales. The flat lizards have greatly flattened bodies and have few if any spiny scales. The grass and snake lizards have tiny, barely usable limbs that look more like little spines than arms and legs. These lizards slither like snakes.

Many species of plated and girdled lizards are drab-colored and blend into the background. In others, the females and juveniles are dull, but the adult males are brightly and beautifully colored. The girdle-tailed and flat lizards range from 5 to 13 inches (13 to 33 centimeters) in length from head to tail tip; adult grass lizards grow to about 22 inches (56 centimeters) in length, and adult plated lizards reach from 6 to 28 inches (15 to 71 centimeters) in total length.

GEOGRAPHIC RANGE

These lizards live in southern Africa and in Madagascar.

HABITAT

The flat and girdle-tailed lizards, along with many plated lizards, typically make their homes in rocky, dry areas, although

phylum

class

subclass

order

monotypic order

suborder

▲ **family**

LIZARD DEFENSE

Although lizards are very good at running away to a safe hiding place, predators (PREH-duh-ters) or those animals that hunt them for food occasionally are able to capture one. Many lizards defend themselves by losing their tails — purposely dropping them — and later growing a new one. Most lizards can still run very quickly without their tails and dash for cover while the predator snacks on the discarded tail. Snake and grass lizards also drop their tails quickly when they are attacked, but then they have another problem. Because these lizards do not have working arms and legs, and rely on the tail to slither around, they are quite helpless until the new tail grows in.

some girdle-tailed lizards live in forests where they hide under tree bark or in tunnels. Grass lizards live in grasslands, and plated lizards prefer more shrubby habitats. One species of plated lizard even survives in the sand dunes of a desert, while another lives on the banks of freshwater rivers.

DIET

The species in this family eat almost anything that they can find or catch. The flat and girdle-tailed lizards hunt by ambush, which means that they lie in wait for an insect to wander by. When the insect or other invertebrate (in-VER-teh-breht), which is an animal without a backbone, comes close enough, they rush out to nab it. They will also eat berries and leaves. The plated lizards are not ambush hunters. Instead, they root around through the soil and piles of leaves to find their meals, which are usually invertebrates. Although they can be quite large animals, the plated lizards move very slowly. Nonetheless, they are able to capture small snakes and lizards occasionally for a bigger meal.

BEHAVIOR AND REPRODUCTION

Girdle-tailed lizards, which are all active during the day, are known for the way they defend themselves. When one feels threatened, it scurries into a crack in a rock, blows up its body, and wedges itself in so an attacker cannot reach it. All of the girdle-tailed lizards have very thick scales. When one species, known as the armadillo lizard, is caught too far from a hiding place, it defends itself by rolling into a ball, even grabbing hold of its tail with its teeth, so that the lizard becomes a difficult-to-swallow, scale-covered ball.

When flat lizards feel threatened, their body shape allows them to slide into very thin cracks in rocks and out of harm's way. Snake and grass lizards avoid predators with their speed. Although they don't have legs to help them run, they can move very quickly through the grass, sometimes boosting themselves along by pushing off with their long tails. When an attacker grabs the tail, a snake or grass lizard simply drops it and grows a new one.

One of the most unusual behaviors of the plated lizards is that they sunbathe, or bask, in an odd position. They lay on the belly with their arms and legs held up in the air. When frightened, which happens quite often for this shy species, they quickly run for cover under a bush or in some other hiding place or bury themselves in loose soil by moving their arms and legs as if they were swimming. Sometimes they will stay underground for 24 hours before coming above ground again.

Many species of girdled lizards live in groups for much of the year, but during the breeding season, adult males will set up territories and fight to keep other males away. In many species, these battles are little more than showdowns where the males display their bright belly colors. Female girdle-tailed, snake, and grass lizards give birth to baby lizards instead of laying eggs. Each year, the typical female has one to twelve young, which are old enough to have young of their own when they reach two to four years old. The flat lizards, on the other hand, lay two eggs each year in a damp spot within a rock crack. Unlike the girdled lizards, only a few species of plated lizards live in small groups: Most live alone. Also unlike the girdled lizards, the plated lizards are all egg-layers. Scientists still know little about the details on most species of plated lizards.

GIRDLED AND PLATED LIZARDS AND PEOPLE

Many species are easily frightened and are therefore rarely seen up close by humans. The less-shy lizards, especially the groups of colorful flat lizards, however, make for excellent viewing at parks and other spots in southern Africa.

CONSERVATION STATUS

According to the World Conservation Union (IUCN), one species of plated lizard is Extinct, which means that it is no longer in existence. Only two specimens of this lizard, called the Eastwood's long-tailed seps, are known. In addition, five species of plated and girdled lizards are Vulnerable, which means that they face a high risk of extinction in the wild, and five species are Near Threatened, which means that they are likely to qualify for a threatened category in the near future. Many of them live in tiny areas that are now being developed for other uses. A number of the lizards are also very beautiful, which has made them quite desirable for the pet trade.

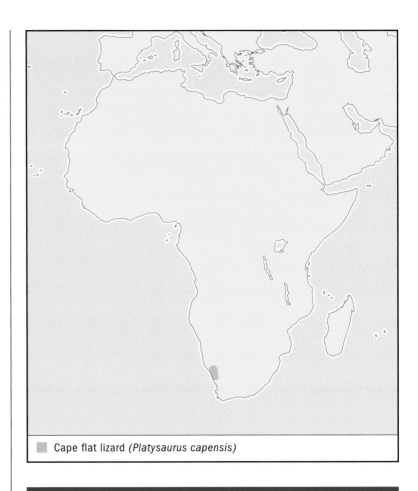

Cape flat lizard (*Platysaurus capensis*)

CAPE FLAT LIZARD
Platysaurus capensis

Physical characteristics: True to their name, the cape flat lizards are very flat animals. The females and juveniles both have a dark brown back with three wide, whitish stripes that run from head to tail. Their bellies are white with a black blotch in the middle. Adult males are much different. The front half of the upper body is bright blue, sometimes with pale spots or stripes, and the back half, including the tail, is brick-red. On the underside, the throat is light blue; the chest, dark blue, and the belly has a black center blotch. Adults range from about 2.5 to 3.3 inches (6.4 to 8.4 centimeters) from the tip of the snout to the vent, which is a slit-like opening on

the underside of the lizard at the beginning of the tail. The tail doubles the overall size, for a total length of about 5 to 6.6 inches (12.8 to 16.8 centimeters).

Geographic range: The cape flat lizard lives in the far southwest portion of Africa, in both South Africa and Namibia.

Habitat: They live in those areas of desert that have many rocks.

Diet: This lizard hunts by ambush, laying in wait in a shady spot under a rock until an insect happens by. At that point, it rushes out to nab the insect for a meal. It also eats flowers and berries when they are available.

Behavior and reproduction: Cape flat lizards are shy animals that run for cover when humans or other potential predators come too close. People usually see them from a distance on top of rocks, especially granite ledges. They may live in small groups. Females lay eggs in November or December and sometimes again a couple of months later. Each time, she lays two large eggs in moist soil beneath or in the crack of a rock.

Cape flat lizards and people: Because they live in deserts away from humans, lizards and humans rarely bother one another.

Conservation status: This species is not listed as endangered or threatened. ■

FOR MORE INFORMATION

Books

Badger, D. *Lizards: A Natural History of Some Uncommon Creatures—Extraordinary Chameleons, Iguanas, Geckos, and More.* Stillwater. MN: Voyageur Press, 2002.

Branch, Bill. *Field Guide to Snakes and Other Reptiles of Southern Africa.* South Africa: Struik Publishers, 1998.

Glaw, Frank, and Miguel Vences. *Field Guide to the Amphibians and Reptiles of Madagascar.* 2nd ed. Privately printed, 1994.

Mattison, Chris. *Lizards of the World.* New York, NY: Facts on File, 1989.

Web sites

"Cordylids of the Cederberg." Cape Nature Conservation. http://www.capenature.org.za/cederbergproject/html/cordylids.html (accessed on October 18, 2004).

"*Cordylus* spp." Melissa Kaplan's Herp Care Collection. http://www.anapsid.org/cordylus.html (accessed on October 18, 2004).

"Plated lizards." Melissa Kaplan's Herp Care Collection. http://www.anapsid.org/plated.html (accessed on October 18, 2004).

"Plated lizards of the Cederberg." Cape Nature Conservation. http://www.capenature.org.za/cederbergproject/html/platedlizards.html (accessed on October 18, 2004).

SKINKS

Scincidae

Class: Reptilia

Order: Squamata

Suborder: Sauria

Family: Scincidae

Number of species: About 1,400 species

family

C H A P T E R

PHYSICAL CHARACTERISTICS

With about 1,400 species, the skinks come in many different sizes, shapes, and colors, but they do share a few features. Members of this family have large head scales, body scales that have bony plates underneath them, and a roof of the mouth that is made of two, flat bony plates instead of one, as humans and other animals have. The bony plate is called a palate (PAL-iht).

The skinks are divided into four major groups or subfamilies. The seventeen species in two of the subfamilies are legless, while the hundreds of species in the other two subfamilies have legs. A few species, known as comb-eared skinks, have noticeable scales that stick out near the ear opening on the side of the head.

Skinks, most of which have smooth scales, may be either small or large. The smallest adults grow to just 0.9 inches (2.3 centimeters) long from the tip of the head to the vent, which is a slit-like opening on the belly side of the lizard. If the lizard has legs, the vent is located between them. The longest skink is 20 times larger than the smallest, reaching 19.3 inches (49 centimeters) from the snout to the vent.

Color varies among the skinks, but many have rather drab, brownish bodies. The males of numerous species, however, often develop colorful heads during the breeding season. In many species, juveniles have bright blue, red, or yellow tails, which are believed to help them escape attacks by predators (PREH-dih-ters), or animals that hunt them for food. The predator snaps at the colored tail, which the young skink drops before running away. Adults are also able to lose their tails and survive.

phylum

class

subclass

order

monotypic order

suborder

▲ **family**

GEOGRAPHIC RANGE

They live on land almost around the world, except for many islands in the ocean and very cold places, such as Antarctica and high up in mountains.

HABITAT

Many skinks live mostly underground, hidden beneath logs, rocks, or among piles of leaves and twigs. Many of those that live underground dig their own burrows. The night skink builds a large tunnel system, which is marked by a large pile of sand near the most-used entrance. This lizard often has to share its tunnels with other animals that drop in day and night to sleep or to escape the weather or a predator. Some other species of skinks are good climbers and spend time on tree branches and tree trunks. While most of them live on land, some do not mind taking a dip in the water. Several species, like Gray's water skink and the eastern water skink, spend part of their time in ponds or streams.

DIET

Most species enjoy insects. Some are rather picky eaters and prefer to eat one kind of insect. Some of the underground-living, legless skinks, for example, eat mostly termites. A few species of skinks, including bobtails and sandfish, mix some flowers and grains into their insect diets, and others, such as the prehensile-tailed skink, are strictly vegetarian.

BEHAVIOR AND REPRODUCTION

Many of the skinks are active during the day, spending much of their days looking for food and sunbathing, or basking. Some species, such as the well-named night skink, only come out in the darkness. Most skinks are nervous animals that take cover if they feel even slightly threatened. For this reason, people often have only short glimpses of them before the lizards dart into a pile of brush or under a log. If an attacker is able to catch a skink before it can take cover, many of the species drop the tail, which continues to wiggle for several minutes. This draws the attention of the attacker and allows the lizard to escape. When the coast is clear, some skinks will return to whatever is left of the tail and eat it themselves. The tail grows back, but it is typically not as long as the original tail. The bobtail is unusual among skinks in that it does not immediately flee when a predator arrives. Instead, this slow-moving lizard stands its ground, opens wide its mouth, and flaps its bright blue tongue.

Skinks do not pant as other lizards do, and scientists think that their extra palate is the reason why. Other lizards pant to cool off. The air they draw in and breathe out when panting cools off the blood in blood vessels along the roof of the mouth. The extra palate in skinks, however, may cover up the blood vessels so much that the air cannot get close enough to cool the blood, making panting useless. Instead, these lizards beat the heat by resting in a shady spot or cool underground burrow.

During mating season, males of many species will fight, biting one another on the head, neck, and tail until one gives up and leaves. In some species, male-female pairs remain together from year to year. Females of some species lay eggs, but other females give birth to baby skinks. Strangely, two species of skinks from Australia—Bougainville's skink and the three-toed skink—do both. Among skinks, the number of young varies from species to species, with some females having only one or two eggs or young at a time, and others having up to sixty-seven. Although most females make their own individual nests, mothers in a few species lay their eggs together in one big nest. Whether they nest together or alone, parents of many species provide some care to their eggs and young.

IN THE BLINK OF AN EYE

When a person blinks, the upper lid slides down over the eye. When a lizard blinks its eye, only the lower eyelid moves. Skinks have a number of different lower eyelids, including some see-through types. These look rather like contact lenses that slide up and cover the eye. In some skinks, their lower eyelids always stay shut. These eyelids have a clear area or are completely clear, so the skinks can see even though their eyes are always closed.

SKINKS AND PEOPLE

Some people keep the larger species as pets, but this family's biggest contribution to people comes when they are left in the wild. Skinks eat many insects, including those considered to be pest species.

CONSERVATION STATUS

According to the World Conservation Union (IUCN), three species are Extinct, which means they are no longer in existence. Twenty-six others are listed as Critically Endangered, Endangered, or Vulnerable, which means they face an extremely high, very high, or high risk of extinction in the wild. Five are Near Threatened and are likely to qualify for a threatened category in the near future; and seven are Data Deficient, which means scientists need more information before they can make a judgment about the threat of extinction. The U.S. Fish and Wildlife Service lists three skinks as Threatened or likely to become endangered in the foreseeable future: the Round Island, bluetail mole, and sand skinks.

Prehensile-tailed skink (*Corucia zebrata*)

PREHENSILE-TAILED SKINK
Corucia zebrata

Physical characteristics: Large in size, the prehensile-tailed skink can grow to 30 inches (76 centimeters) in length from head to tail. A prehensile (pri-HEN-sihl) tail is one adapted for grasping like a monkey's tail. It has a muscular tail, a large head, and clawed legs on a thick grayish to brownish green body. Its underside is lighter green. The males usually are a bit thinner than the females and have a slightly bigger head.

Geographic range: They live east of New Guinea on the Solomon Islands.

Habitat: Prehensile-tailed skinks spend much of their days hidden among the leaves high up in trees, especially the strangler fig tree, or

in holes in tree trunks or branches. They become active at night when they look for food.

Diet: Unlike the vast majority of other skinks, this species is a strict vegetarian and particularly likes leaves and flowers it finds in the trees.

Behavior and reproduction: Active at night, this skink usually spends its time slowly and calmly climbing on tree branches. When it feels threatened, it will hiss and even bite if necessary. Females usually give birth to just one baby at a time.

Prehensile-tailed skinks and people: Native people eat this skink. Other people often see them in zoos or other lizard exhibits, and some keep them as pets.

Conservation status: Although the prehensile-tailed skink is not listed as endangered or threatened, it faces a serious threat from over-collection by the pet trade. ■

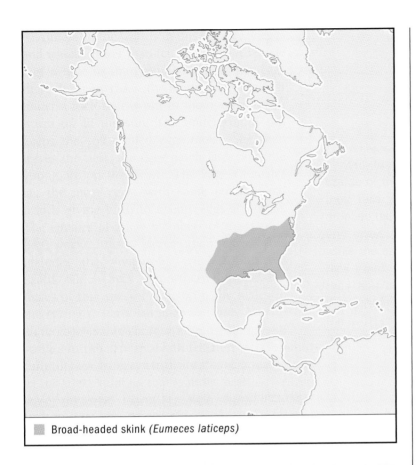

Broad-headed skink (*Eumeces laticeps*)

BROAD-HEADED SKINK
Eumeces laticeps

Physical characteristics: Also known as the greater five-lined skink, the broad-headed skink is a brown to brownish gray lizard with darker, although often faint, stripes running from its wide head to the tail. The head of males turns reddish during the mating season. Adults grow to 9.8 inches (25 centimeters) in length.

Geographic range: Broad-headed skinks live mainly in the southeastern quarter of the United States.

Habitat: An excellent climber, the broad-headed skink lives in a variety of areas, including swamps, forests, and even near people, in everything from farm buildings to trash-filled city lots.

Diet: They spend much of their time looking for insects and other invertebrates (in-VER-teh-brehts), which are animals without backbones, to eat.

Behavior and reproduction: When broad-headed skinks feel threatened, which is quite often for these shy lizards, they quickly dart away. During the breeding season, males jump at and bite each other on the head, neck, or tail. Before long, one of the two fighting lizards will surrender and leave, and the other is left to mate with a female. Females lay six to ten eggs at a time under leaves or in some other hiding spot and stay with them until they hatch.

Broad-headed skinks and people: Most people see these lizards from a distance as they climb along fences or walk along tree branches. They are very shy and run when approached, so people rarely get a close look.

Conservation status: This species is not considered endangered or threatened. ■

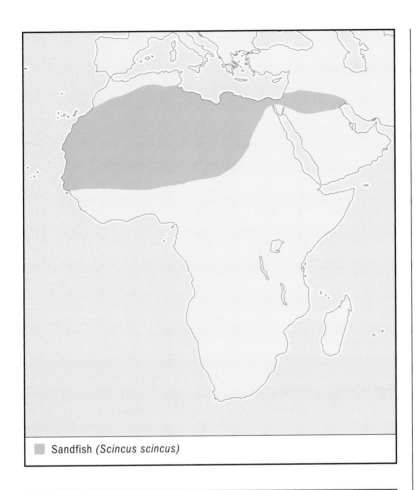

Sandfish (*Scincus scincus*)

SANDFISH
Scincus scincus

Physical characteristics: Sandfish are light brown lizards with slightly darker brown bands down the back. They have a pointed snout and thin legs ending in fringed toes that help them run on shifting sands. Adult sandfish usually reach about 8 inches (20.3 centimeters) in length, including the short tail.

Geographic range: Sandfish can be found in northern Africa, Iraq, Iran, Israel, and Jordan.

Habitat: Although they live in deserts, sandfish tend to live near a moister area, such as an oasis, which has loose sand and many plants.

When it feels threatened, the sandfish dives headfirst into the sandy ground and swims below the surface of the sand. (Illustration by Barbara Duperron. Reproduced by permission.)

Diet: Sandfish eat insects, scorpions, and other invertebrates, and an occasional small lizard. They move their arms and legs in a motion that allows them to "swim" through and just below the surface of the sand. From this position, they snatch unsuspecting insects walking on the ground above them. They also eat flowers and grains.

Behavior and reproduction: Active during the day, this lizard is best known for the way it escapes attackers. When it feels threatened, the sandfish dives headfirst into the sandy ground and swims below the surface of the sand. After a June breeding season, female sandfish lay about six eggs.

Sandfish and people: Native people hunt sandfish for their meat. At one time, people believed that dead dried sandfish could cure various diseases.

Conservation status: This species is not considered endangered or threatened. ■

FOR MORE INFORMATION

Books

Badger, D. *Lizards: A Natural History of Some Uncommon Creatures—Extraordinary Chameleons, Iguanas, Geckos, and More.* Stillwater, MN: Voyageur Press, 2002.

Greer, Allen E. *The Biology and Evolution of Australian Lizards.* Chipping Norton, Australia: Surrey Beatty and Sons, 1989.

Hutchinson, M. N. "Family Scincidae." In *Fauna of Australia.* Vol. 2A, *Amphibia and Reptilia,* edited by C. J. Gasby, C. J. Ross, and P. L. Beesly. Canberra: Australian Biological and Environmental Survey, 1993.

Mattison, Chris. *Lizards of the World.* New York, NY: Facts on File, 1989.

Pianka, E. R. *Ecology and Natural History of Desert Lizards: Analyses of the Ecological Niche and Community Structure.* Princeton, NJ: Princeton University Press, 1986.

Pianka, E. R., and L. J. Vitt. *Lizards: Windows to the Evolution of Diversity.* Berkeley: University of California Press, 2003.

Storr, G. M., L. A. Smith, and R. E. Johnstone. *Lizards of Western Australia.* Vol. 1, *Skinks.* Perth: Western Australian Museum, 1999.

Periodicals

"Black Market Animals: The Stealing, Smuggling and Selling of Endangered Species as Pets is a $10 Billion Illegal Business Worldwide." *Current Events*, a Weekly Reader publication (April 14, 1997): 2A.

Geschickter, Jacqueline. "Say Ahhhh!" *National Geographic World* (November 2000): 31.

Thompson, Sharon. "Attention, Lizard Parents!" *National Geographic World* (May 2002): 6.

Web sites

"Blue-tongued Skink." *Enchanted Learning.* http://www.enchantedlearning. com/subjects/reptiles/lizard/Bluetonguedskink.shtml (accessed on November 3, 2004).

"Eastern Water Skink." Australian Museum. http://www.amonline.net .au/wild_kids/freshwater/water_skink.htm (accessed on November 3, 2004).

"Many-lined Skink." Yahooligans! Animals. http://yahooligans.yahoo. com/content/animals/species/4414.html (accessed on November 3, 2004).

Vanwormer, E. 2002. "*Eumeces fasciatus* (five-lined skink)." Animal Diversity Web, University of Michigan Museum of Zoology. http:// animaldiversity.ummz.umich.edu/site/accounts/information/Eumeces_ fasciatus.html (accessed on November 03, 2004).

Other sources

McCoy, Mike. *Reptiles of the Solomon Islands.* CD-ROM. Kuranda, Australia: ZooGraphics, 2000.

family
CHAPTER

PHYSICAL CHARACTERISTICS

This family contains four groups of lizards: the glass lizards and slowworms, the legless lizards, the galliwasps, and the alligator lizards. Many of these species in the Anguidae family have bodies that are nearly all brown, but some are green, and others have stripes or bands. The glass lizards have especially shiny scales. In a few species, the males are more brightly colored than the females. Among alligator lizards that live in mountainous areas, for example, the females and the juveniles are a drab brown, and the males are bright green or yellowish green. Some, such as the La Selle galliwasp, are small and reach only about 2.8 inches (7 centimeters) in length from head to tail tip. The slowworm, on the other hand, can grow to nearly 20 times that size at 55.1 inches (140 centimeters) long.

In general, the scales of these species are thick and strong, giving them an armor-like covering. Many of the legless lizards and galliwasps have a fold on each side of the body, which allows their bodies to stretch out when they eat a particularly big meal or when a female is pregnant. Some of the species, including the legless lizards, have no limbs and therefore slither about with a twisting motion. A few, such as the Moroccan glass lizard, have no front legs but do have tiny hind legs that look like small flaps located near the vent, which is a slitlike opening on the underside of the animal. The tail in galliwasps, legless lizards, and alligator lizards is usually shorter than the rest of the body, but the tail is far longer than the body in glass lizards. In all lizards, including those without legs, the tail begins at the vent. A few species, such as the Cuban alligator lizard, live in trees and have tails that can wrap around and cling to branches and twigs. In addition, many members of this family have eyelids that they noticeably blink open and shut.

GEOGRAPHIC RANGE

These lizards live in North, Central, and South America, Europe, and Asia. They also make their homes on many islands of the West Indies. One species, the Moroccan glass lizard, lives in northern Africa.

HABITAT

Most of these lizards live on land and on the ground's surface, but they often remain in leaf piles, under stones, or in some other hiding spot. A few make their homes underground, and some spend much of their time in trees. While many species live in moist, low-lying areas, some live high in mountain forests or in dry and shrubby deserts.

DIET

These lizards will eat a number of different animals. They typically move very slowly, so their diet includes other slow-traveling things, such as snails, slugs, spiders, some insects, and other invertebrates (in-VER-teh-brehts), which are animals without backbones. When they eat vertebrates (VER-teh-brehts), which are animals with backbones, they tend to dine on bird eggs, baby rodents that are still in the nest, or other small animals, such as salamanders, that are not fast enough to get away.

BEHAVIOR AND REPRODUCTION

Depending on the species, they may be active during the day or at night. They usually stay out of sight, but many species will come out into the open on a sunny day to soak up the warmth. Such sunbathing is called basking. Often, these shy lizards will only expose one part of their bodies at a time while basking, keeping the rest hidden away. Those species that live in colder areas may spend the winter in a deep sleep, known as hibernation (high-bur-NAY-shun).

These lizards are especially known for their behavior when they feel threatened: Most members of this family quickly drop the tail, which may break into several wriggling pieces. While the attacker is looking at or eating the tail, the lizard makes its escape.

The lizard grows back the tail, but it is often much shorter than the original one. The glass lizard's regrown tail, for example, is a pointed stump. Some lizards in this family will also defend themselves by wiggling frantically, by smearing a bad-smelling ooze and/or feces on the attacker, or by puffing up the body with air, which may make the lizard appear large enough to scare off an attacker.

Within this family, some species lay eggs and others give birth to baby lizards. Female legless lizards all have one or two live babies in each litter. Depending on the species, female glass lizards and slowworms, galliwasps, and alligator lizards may lay eggs or give birth to baby lizards, with brood sizes from less than five to two dozen or more. In some egg-laying species, the female stays with the eggs, often wrapping her body around them, until they hatch. Most species have young every year, but some, such as the montane alligator lizard, probably only give birth once every two years. During breeding season, males of some species, including the slowworm, will fight by grasping at one another with their jaws. For most species, however, scientists know little about their courtship behaviors.

ALLIGATOR LIZARDS, GALLIWASPS, THEIR RELATIVES, AND PEOPLE

Because many species like to hide, people rarely see them in the wild unless a person is plowing a field or raking leaves in their habitat. Some people mistake the glass lizard's stubby and pointed regrown tail for a stinger, but all lizards in this family are harmless. Several species are fairly common in the pet trade.

CONSERVATION STATUS

According to the World Conservation Union (IUCN), one species is Extinct, which means that it is no longer in existence. This species, the Jamaica giant galliwasp, was last seen in 1840. It probably disappeared because people brought new species, including the mongoose, to Jamaica to kill rats. The mongoose, however, also eats galliwasps and probably played a role in their extinction. In addition, the IUCN names three species as Critically Endangered, which means they face an extremely high risk of extinction in the wild; one species as Endangered, which means it faces a very high risk of extinction in the wild, and one species as Vulnerable, which means it faces a high risk of extinction in the wild. These and other unlisted species are threatened by habitat destruction, particularly in such small places as the islands of the West Indies. The IUCN also lists three species as Data Deficient, which means that scientists have too little information to make a judgment about the threat of extinction.

Texas alligator lizard (*Gerrhonotus liocephalus*)

TEXAS ALLIGATOR LIZARD
Gerrhonotus liocephalus

Physical characteristics: The Texas alligator lizard has a long tail and, unlike some other members of this family, four working legs. Its squarish scales somewhat resemble those of an alligator. Its back is reddish brown, sometimes yellowish, with crooked crossbands of white and black scales. Adults usually range from 9.8 to 15.7 inches (25 to 40 centimeters) in length, but some can be as long as 19.7 inches (50 centimeters).

Geographic range: They live from Texas in the United States to San Luis Potosí in central Mexico.

Habitat: The Texas alligator lizard often lives on rocky hillsides, preferring areas without many plants, although it does sometimes live in dry woods and shrubby areas.

Diet: This slow-moving species spends much of the day searching for various invertebrates, as well as small rodents or other vertebrates, it can capture and eat.

Behavior and reproduction: This species is active during the day. When it feels threatened, it can blow itself up with air, which may make it appear large enough that a predator will leave it alone. Females lay five to thirty-one eggs at least once a year, and they often remain with the eggs until they hatch.

Texas alligator lizards and people: People sometimes collect these lizards for pets.

Conservation status: The Texas alligator lizard is not listed as endangered or threatened. ■

FOR MORE INFORMATION

Books

Badger, D. *Lizards: A Natural History of Some Uncommon Creatures—Extraordinary Chameleons, Iguanas, Geckos, and More.* Stillwater, MN: Voyageur Press, 2002.

Capula, Massimo. *Simon and Schuster's Guide to Reptiles and Amphibians of the World.* New York: Simon and Schuster, 1989.

Grismer, L. Lee. *Amphibians and Reptiles of Baja California, Including Its Pacific Islands and the Islands in the Sea of Cortés.* Berkeley: University of California Press, 2002.

Mattison, Chris. *Lizards of the World.* New York, NY: Facts on File, 1989.

Savage, Jay M. *The Amphibians and Reptiles of Costa Rica.* Chicago: University of Chicago Press, 2002.

Web sites

"Alligator Lizard." Melissa Kaplan's Herp Care Collection. http://www.anapsid.org/gerrhont.html (accessed on October 20, 2004).

"Eastern Glass Lizard." Yahooligans! Animals. http://yahooligans.yahoo.com/ content/animals/species/4313.html (accessed on October 20, 2004).

"Glass Lizard - Glass Snake - Legless Lizard." Melissa Kaplan's Herp Care Collection. http://www.anapsid.org/legless.html (accessed on October 20, 2004).

"Northern Alligator Lizard." Yahooligans! Animals. http://yahooligans.yahoo.com/content/animals/species/4322.html (accessed on October 20, 2004).

"Slender Glass Lizard." Iowa Herpetology. http://www.herpnet.net/Iowa-Herpetology/reptiles/lizards/glass_lizard.html(accessed on October 20, 2004).

Class: Reptilia

Order: Squamata

Suborder: Lacertilia

Family: Xenosauridae

Number of species: 6 species

family

C H A P T E R

PHYSICAL CHARACTERISTICS

With their flat heads and bodies and lumpy scales, the knob-scaled lizards have an unusual look. The head is usually triangular in shape, coming to a point at the tip of the snout. Some have a very noticeable ridge above the eye and extending forward to the snout and backward to the rear of the head. Often, the females have larger bodies than the males, but the males typically have bigger heads. Their bodies are usually dark brown to black, often with lighter-colored bands or blotches. The largest specimens grow to 4.7 to 5.1 inches (12 to 13 centimeters) long from the tip of the snout to the vent, a slitlike opening on the belly side of the animal at the beginning of the tail. The tail stretches nearly as long as the body.

Until 1999, this family only had four species. Discoveries of two new species—one in 2000 and one in 2002—increased the number to six. The two new species are known only by their scientific names: *Xenosaurus penai* and *Xenosaurus phalaroantheron*. Scientists believe additional species are yet to be identified. In particular, they suspect that a closer look at some of the already known knob-scaled lizards may reveal that they should actually be separated into two or more similar-looking species. This type of splitting is especially common in animals that live in small groups that are separated from one another, so the individuals from one group, or population, never see individuals from another population.

GEOGRAPHIC RANGE

Knob-scaled lizards live in typically small populations widely scattered from the Tamaulipas in northeastern Mexico on the

phylum

class

subclass

order

monotypic order

suborder

▲ **family**

Gulf of Mexico south to the middle of Guatemala in Central America.

HABITAT

Most knob-scaled lizards live in the mountains. Some species make their homes in cool cloud forests, while others prefer drier climates and live in hot, shrubby areas. In both cases, the knob-scaled lizards take advantage of their flattened shape and seek out cracks and holes in rocks and bark and other hiding places, where they spend much of their lives.

At one time, scientists included the Chinese crocodile lizard in this family. This lizard is now in its own family. Unlike the knob-scaled lizards, the Chinese crocodile lizard lives most of its life in or near shallow forest ponds, where it eats tadpoles and fishes.

DIET

These lizards are ambush hunters, which means that they sit very still and wait for their meal to come to them. Their meals are usually made up of insects that happen to come too close to their hiding places, which are usually in rock crevices. The lizards quickly grab the insects and gulp them down. Like other lizards, these species flick their tongues to pick up chemical odors from their insect prey. They cannot smell with their tongues, but they can smell with a special organ, called a Jacobson's organ, that sits above a small opening on the roof of the mouth. The lizard picks up the chemicals with its tongue and places them on the opening. A study of tongue-flicking behavior in *Xenosaurus platyceps* found that the young ones flicked their tongues to smell prey whether the lizards were in their hiding places or not, while the adult lizards did most of their tongue-flicking only when they were in holes or cracks. In other words, the adults were much more interested in finding prey when they were out of sight than when they were in the open.

At least one species of knob-scaled lizards, the Newman's knob-scaled lizard, will also eat bits of plants and some mammal meat. This suggests that the lizards may prefer insects but will eat just about anything they can find. Scientists call such animals opportunistic (ah-por-toon-ISS-tik), because they include almost any kind of plant or animal in their diet—if they are hungry and the opportunity presents itself.

BEHAVIOR AND REPRODUCTION

These lizards stay hidden away most of the time. Individuals in some species, including the one known simply as the knob-scaled lizard, live alone and defend their homes. Males will even bite one another on the head, which can leave behind noticeable scars. Other species, like Newman's knob-scaled lizard, are much more welcoming. In this species, pairs of male and female lizards often live together in peace in the same crevices. Members of this family usually stay in the same area throughout their lives, which can be quite long. Newman's knob-scaled lizards, for example, can live to be at least seven years old.

Females in all species give birth to baby lizards, rather than laying eggs as many other lizards do. A typical clutch for a lizard from this family is one to three babies, but some of those in the knob-scaled lizard species can have six young at a time. Once the females have their babies, usually from June to August, some stay with their young. Scientists have found that mothers in Newman's knob-scaled lizard species and the species known as *Xenosaurus platyceps* remain with their babies in their hidden-away homes, often keeping the young farther inside the hole or crevice, while the mothers stay nearer the entrance as if guarding the babies from possible land predators.

Some reports indicate that the lizards are most active at dawn and dusk and during the night. Because populations are scattered, their numbers are low, and they usually stay out of sight, much about their behavior and reproduction is still unknown.

KNOB-SCALED LIZARDS AND PEOPLE

At least one population of Newman's knob-scaled lizard lives in the cracks of a rock wall on a plantation, but for the most part the lizards in this family and people hardly ever see one another. Since the lizards seem to make their homes in very small areas and travel very little from those areas, however, farming or other human activity that might destroy their habitat

REALLY RELATED?

Many scientists once included the Chinese crocodile lizard as one of the species in the family of knob-scaled lizards. The Chinese crocodile lizard is very similar in appearance to the other knob-scaled lizards, which all live in Mexico and Central America. A 1999 study, however, compared their DNA and found that the Chinese crocodile lizard is different enough to have its own family, which is now called Shinisauridae. DNA is genetic material, essentially, an instruction booklet for making a living thing, that is passed down from parents to babies. By looking at differences in these "instructions," scientists can tell how closely two species are related.

could mean disaster for the lizards, which would likely be unable to find a new home nearby.

CONSERVATION STATUS

Although scientists still know little about these species or their overall population sizes, they are not considered endangered or threatened.

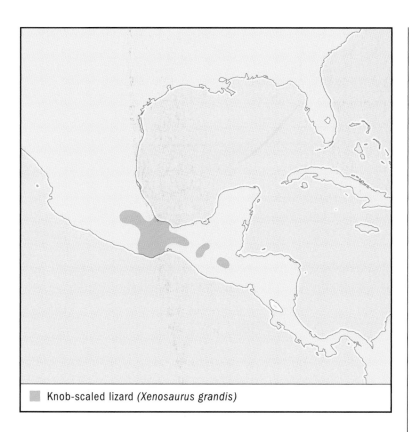

Knob-scaled lizard *(Xenosaurus grandis)*

KNOB-SCALED LIZARD
Xenosaurus grandis

Physical characteristics: With a flat head and body and tall, bumpy scales, the knob-scaled lizard looks much like the other lizards in this family. This species, however, has bright red eyes and usually a dark-brown body, often with tan to cream bands or blotches. It grows to about 10 inches (25 centimeters) long from the tip of its snout to the end of its tail. The tail is a bit shorter than the rest of the body. Males and females are about the same size.

Geographic range: The knob-scaled lizard lives in both Central America and Mexico, stretching from Guatemala in the south to Veracruz, Mexico, on the Gulf of Mexico in the north.

Habitat: This species lives in wooded areas containing numerous cracks and crevices in rocks and bark where they can remain out of sight.

The knob-tailed lizard has bright red eyes and a usually dark-brown body, often with tan to cream bands or blotches. (Illustration by Brian Cressman. Reproduced by permission.)

Diet: Like other species in this family, the knob-scaled lizard mainly eats insects, which it captures by ambush.

Behavior and reproduction: These lizards typically live alone in their crevices, which they defend against other members of their species. Male-to-male fights sometimes break out, with the males biting at one another's head. Females give birth to one to six baby lizards at a time.

Knob-scaled lizards and people: Knob-scaled lizards and people rarely see or bother one another.

Conservation status: Although much about this species is unknown, it is not considered endangered or threatened. ■

FOR MORE INFORMATION

Books:

Halliday, Tim, and Kraig Adler, eds. *The Encyclopedia of Reptiles and Amphibians.* New York, NY: Facts on File, 1986.

Mattison, Chris. *Lizards of the World.* New York, NY: Facts on File, 1989.

Web sites:

"Chinese Crocodile Lizard." Center for Research on Concepts and Cognition, Indiana University. http://www.cogsci.indiana.edu/farg/harry/bio/zoo/shinisau.htm (accessed on December 8, 2004).

"Xenosauridae." Animal Diversity Web. http://animaldiversity. ummz.umich .edu/site/accounts/information/Xenosauridae.html (accessed on November 16, 2004).

"Xenosauridae." Virtual Museum of Natural History. http://www.curator .org/LegacyVMNH/WebOfLife/Kingdom/P_Chordata/ClassReptilia/ O_Squamata/InfraAnguimorphan/SupFDiploglossa/FXenosauridae/ xenosauridae.htm (accessed on December 8, 2004).

GILA MONSTER AND MEXICAN
BEADED LIZARD
Helodermatidae

Class: Reptilia

Order: Squamata

Suborder: Scleroglossa

Family: Helodermatidae

Number of species: 2 species

family

CHAPTER

PHYSICAL CHARACTERISTICS

The two species in this family, the Gila monster and the Mexican beaded lizard, are both large, heavy-bodied lizards coated with small, rounded bumps that look like the beadwork on clothing. The bumps, which are actually pebblelike scales, cover the tops of the arms, legs, head, and tail, as well as the back and sides of the body. These lizards have rather short, but strong arms and legs and long, thin claws. The tail may be thin or thick, depending on how well-fed the individual is. This is because these lizards store fat in their tails. Beaded lizards have slightly longer tails than the Gila monsters. An average beaded tail is at least two-thirds the length of the entire body, but the typical Gila tail is about half the total body length. Unlike many other lizards, these two species also have thick, forked tongues. Members of the same species can look very different from one another. Some adults are brightly patterned, while others are faded and dull. The patterns may be made up of spots, blotches, circles, bands, or squiggles on a background of pink, orange, yellow, dark gray, or black. Juveniles are usually banded.

Gila monsters and Mexican beaded lizards are the only two venomous (VEH-nuh-mus) lizards in the world. Unlike venomous snakes that deliver venom from the upper jaw and through grooves in just the two fangs, these lizards store their venom in the lower jaw and deliver it through grooves in numerous teeth.

Adult Gila monsters and beaded lizards range from 12 to 18 inches (30 to 45 centimeters) from the snout to the vent, which

phylum

class

subclass

order

monotypic order

suborder

▲ **family**

LIVING FOSSILS

The Gila monster and Mexican beaded lizard are often called "living fossils." This means that they have changed very little from the way their ancestors looked millions of years ago. Both lizards belong to a family that scientists have traced back 98 million years, long before the great dinosaur extinction of 65 million years ago. Most species in this family have disappeared, but the Gila monster and Mexican beaded lizard remain and display many of the characteristics of their long-gone relatives.

is a difficult-to-see opening on the underside of the lizard at the beginning of the tail, or 14 to 39 inches (35 to 100 centimeters) from the snout to the tip of the tail. They weigh 1.0 to 4.4 pounds (450 grams to 2 kilograms). The beaded lizard can grow larger than the Gila monster.

GEOGRAPHIC RANGE

They live in North and Central America from the southwestern United States to northwestern Mexico, in Guatemala, and also in the state of Chiapas in southern Mexico.

HABITAT

Gila monsters and beaded lizards stay in deserts usually, although some make their homes in dry grassland, in shrubby forests on hillsides, or in nearby areas that have boulders or burrows where they can hide.

DIET

Gila monsters and beaded lizards wander through their habitat looking for young rabbits or rodents or snakes and lizard eggs to eat. They will even climb trees and cacti in search of bird eggs.

BEHAVIOR AND REPRODUCTION

These species spend about twenty-three hours of every day out of sight in burrows, within cracks in rocks, or in trees. When they do travel above ground, they wander about during the day looking for food or for mating partners, sometimes traveling more than 0.6 miles (1 kilometer). They also may come out in the evening. During the breeding season, the males of both species will fight one another, sometimes battling for two or three hours at a time. The male beaded lizards will arch their bodies and wrestle belly-to-belly until one comes out on top. The male Gila monsters wrestle by twisting the body to and fro. Courtship and mating occur in spring for the Gila monsters and in fall for the beaded lizards. Two to three months later, female Gila monsters lay two to twelve eggs, and female beaded lizards lay two to twenty-two eggs. Hatchling Gila monsters leave the nest the following spring in April, and hatchling beaded lizards appear in June or July as the wet season begins.

GILA MONSTERS, MEXICAN BEADED LIZARDS, AND PEOPLE

Although they are venomous, bites to humans are rare and typically only occur when a person tries to pick up one of these normally slow-moving Gila monsters or Mexican beaded lizards. Both can twist around quickly and deliver a hard bite. Their powerful jaws can remain clamped shut on a finger or hand for many minutes. While a bite can cause awful pain, swelling, and sometimes vomiting and sweating, it is hardly ever fatal. In fact, the last death due to a Gila monster bite occurred in 1930. On the positive side, scientists have found that substances in the venom may be useful in treating human diseases, such as diabetes.

CONSERVATION STATUS

The World Conservation Union (IUCN) considers both species in this family as Vulnerable, which means that they face a high risk of extinction in the wild. The destruction of their habitat, particularly as it is developed for housing or other human uses, is one of the biggest reasons they are at risk. Another reason for their low numbers is that humans sometimes illegally collect them for the pet trade or for personal pets.

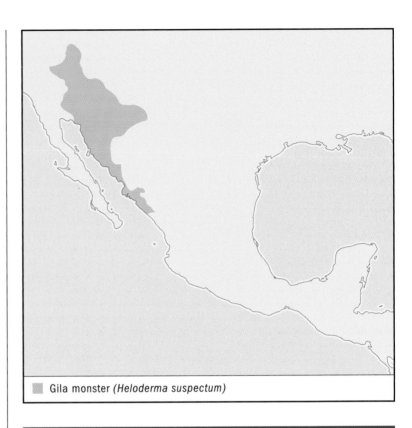

Gila monster (*Heloderma suspectum*)

GILA MONSTER
Heloderma suspectum

Physical characteristics: The Gila monster is a slow-moving, heavy-bodied lizard with rather short, clawed arms and legs and upper skin that looks beaded. The beads are actually rounded scales that appear on the top of the head, back, tail, and limbs and down the sides of the body. The color of the skin and scales differs from individual to individual, but most have at least some pattern, which can be quite bright and beautiful, of squiggles, spots, blotches, circles, and bands. Colors range from pink, orange, and yellow to black and dark gray. Well-fed Gila monsters have thick tails, which store fat. This species and the Mexican beaded lizard are the only two venomous lizards in the world. Adult Gila monsters commonly grow to about 20 inches (50 centimeters) in length from head to tail tip.

Geographic range: The Gila monster makes its home in the southwestern United States and in Sonora, Mexico.

Habitat: Gila monsters live in warm habitats, including deserts, grasslands, and shrubby forests, sometimes on flat ground and sometimes on hillsides. They spend most of their time in underground burrows, inside large cracks in rocks, or in other hiding places, only coming above ground for about one hour a day.

Diet: Gila monsters need to eat only three large meals a year to survive. They store fat in the tail and then use it up between meals, which can be several months apart. Their favorite foods include lizard, snake, and bird eggs, as well as young cottontail rabbits and rodents.

Behavior and reproduction: They remain in burrows or other hiding places for all but about one hour a day when they venture out to look for food or mates. If they feel threatened, they will hiss and sometimes snap at or bite the attacker. Once they bite, they have a very strong grip and may hold it for five minutes or longer. Males and females court and mate from late April to early June, and in July and August the females lay eggs in a damp sand nest. Babies are about 6.5 inches long from snout to tail tip when they hatch.

Gila monsters and people: A Gila monster bite can be painful, but it is almost never fatal to humans. The last reported death from a bite occurred in 1930. Bites rarely happen, however, and usually result from a person's carelessness in picking up the lizard.

Conservation status: The World Conservation Union (IUCN) considers the species to be Vulnerable, which means that it faces a high risk of extinction in the wild. Habitat loss and illegal collection are the main problems the lizards face. ■

FOR MORE INFORMATION

Books

Badger, D. *Lizards: A Natural History of Some Uncommon Creatures—Extraordinary Chameleons, Iguanas, Geckos, and More.* Stillwater, MN: Voyageur Press, 2002.

Brown, David E., and Neil B. Carmony. *Gila Monster: Facts and Folklore of America's Aztec Lizard.* Salt Lake City, UT: University of Utah Press, 1999.

Campbell, Jonathan A., and William W. Lamar. *The Venomous Reptiles of Latin America.* Ithaca, NY: Comstock Publishing Associates, 1989.

Lowe, Charles H., Cecil R. Schwalbe, and Terry B. Johnson. *The Venomous Reptiles of Arizona.* Phoenix: Arizona Game and Fish Department, 1986.

Martin, James, and Joe McDonald. *Poisonous Lizards: Gila Monsters and Mexican Beaded Lizards.* Minneapolis, MN: Capstone Press, 1999.

Mattison, Chris. *Lizards of the World.* New York, NY: Facts on File, 1989.

Web sites

"Gila Monster." Animal Planet: Corwin's Carnival of Creatures. http://animal.discovery.com/fansites/jeffcorwin/carnival/lizard/gilamonster.html (accessed on October 16, 2004).

"Gila Monster." Enchanted Learning. http://www.enchantedlearning.com/subjects/reptiles/lizard/Gilamonster.shtml (accessed on October 16, 2004).

"Gila Monster." WhoZoo. http://www.whozoo.org/anlife2000/jamiebritt/gilaindexrev.html (accessed on November 3, 2004).

"Mexican Beaded Lizard." Lincoln Park Zoo. http://www.lpzoo.com/tour/factsheets/herps/beaded_lizard.html (accessed on October 16, 2004).

**MONITORS, GOANNAS, AND
EARLESS MONITOR**

Varanidae

Class: Reptilia

Order: Squamata

Suborder: Varanoidei

Family: Varanidae

Number of species: About 61
species

family
CHAPTER

phylum

class

subclass

order

monotypic order

suborder

▲ **family**

PHYSICAL CHARACTERISTICS

The monitors, goannas, and earless monitor all have a similar overall appearance, although some are rather small and others are very large. The smallest species is the Australian pygmy monitor that only reaches about 6.7 to 7.9 inches (17 to 20 centimeters) in length from snout to tail tip and weighs just 0.28 to 0.71 ounces (8 to 20 grams). The family contains the largest lizards in the world. The heaviest is the Indonesian Komodo dragon. This immense animal can grow to be at least 9.9 feet (3 meters) long and 330 pounds (150 kilograms). Many people consider the crocodile monitor to be the world's longest lizard. They may grow to 12 feet (nearly 3.7 meters) long from snout to tail tip, or as some reports claim, the lizards can reach a whopping 15 to 19 feet (4.6 to 5.8 meters) in length.

The monitors, goannas, and earless monitor have heavy bodies and long necks. Their tongues are long and forked, and they have noticeable, sometimes large, eyes. Many have somewhat saggy skin that hangs in small folds on their sides and necks. Most of the members of this family have teeth with edges like saw blades, which help them tear through the skin and flesh of their prey.

GEOGRAPHIC RANGE

Australia is home to about one-half of the known species. Members of this family also live in Africa; central to southern mainland Asia; Southeast Asia, especially the Malaysian and Indonesian islands; and Papua, New Guinea.

HABITAT

These lizards live in many different habitats from dry deserts and grasslands, to lush forests and swamps. Some rarely if ever leave the land, and others rarely leave the water. Several species climb trees. This includes the green tree monitor of New Guinea and Australia, which has a very strong tail that it uses when climbing.

DIET

Most members of this family are meat-eaters. The smaller species typically dine on insects, centipedes, worms, and other invertebrates (pronounced in-VER-teh-brehts), which are animals without backbones. Medium-sized species eat lizards, lizard and turtle eggs, and young mammals and birds, while the very large monitors will capture, kill, and eat deer, monkeys, adult birds, wild pigs, buffalo, and other big animals. Monitors also eat carrion (KARE-ree-un), which is the flesh of an already-dead animal. They are not picky eaters, and many will even eat young of their own species. A few species eat fruit.

Members of this family spend a good part of the day looking for food, with some traveling 0.6 mile (1 kilometer) or more between sunup and sunset. They flick their tongues to pick up the scent of a prey animal and then rely on their eyesight and their ears to help hunt down the animal when they get close. Some species, including the sand monitor, swing their heads back and forth while flicking their tongues so they can pick up scents from a wider area and then track animals, especially small lizards, to their underground burrows. They use their long claws to dig up the lizards. Other species, such as the Komodo dragon, sometimes hunt by ambush, which means that they sit very still so they are not obvious and wait for a prey animal to wander by. The Komodo dragon then rushes from its hiding spot and grabs the animal.

BEHAVIOR AND REPRODUCTION

These lizards are active during the day. Those that live on land spend their nights in the hollow of a tree, a burrow that they dig, or some other hiding place. Many of them enter the water at times and are good swimmers. A few, such as the Nile monitor and Merten's water monitor, only come out of the water to sunbathe, or bask, on shore. The females also leave the water to dig holes along the shoreline, where they lay their eggs.

Many species in this family hide themselves when they hear people coming, so people often see little but their footprints. When they cannot hide, these lizards will defend themselves. They will typically flatten out from side to side and puff out their cheeks, which makes them look larger. A few even stand up on their hind legs. They also hiss. Some of the larger species can be quite dangerous, because they can swing their tail around with great speed and use it as a whip to strike the attacker. The Komodo dragon is large enough to kill humans with bites from its powerful jaws.

During the breeding season, males will fight over females. Their fights are wrestling matches in which two males stand belly to belly, grip each other with their arms, and try to knock one another down. Smaller species wrestle while lying on the ground. The winning male then courts the female by flicking his tongue over her snout and body. After mating, the females lay eggs in underground burrows, occasionally dug in the middle of termite nests or ground-built bird nests. Depending on the species, she may lay two to sixty eggs. The smallest species lay the fewest eggs, and the largest lay the most.

GIANT LIZARDS

The Komodo dragon is the heaviest lizard on Earth today, but it is only half as long and weighs just one-quarter of the amount of its ancient relative, known as *Megalania prisca*. This enormous lizard tipped the scales at more than 1,320 pounds (600 kilograms), compared to the Komodo's 330 pounds (150 kilograms). While a Komodo can grow to an impressive 10 feet long (3 meters), *Megalania prisca* grew to at least 20 feet (6.1 meters) from snout to tail tip. Some people believe it may have even reached 30 feet (9.1 meters) or more. Now extinct, the lizard lived until at least 19,000 years ago.

MONITORS, GOANNAS, EARLESS MONITOR, AND PEOPLE

These lizards are usually shy animals that hide when people approach. For this reason, people usually do not see them. The footprints they leave behind, however, usually provide enough clues to tell which species recently passed by. Monitor lizards are often mentioned in ancient tales and are likely the basis for legends of dragons. Some humans now hunt them for their skin, which is highly prized as leather.

CONSERVATION STATUS

According to the World Conservation Union (IUCN), two species are Vulnerable, which means they face a high risk of extinction in the wild. These are the Indonesian Komodo dragon and the Philippine Gray's monitor. Their low numbers are due mainly to habitat loss and to hunting. People kill these lizards for their skin. The U.S. Fish and Wildlife Service lists the following four species as Endangered, which means that they are in danger of extinction throughout all or a significant portion of their range: the desert monitor, the Indian monitor, the Komodo dragon, and the yellow monitor.

Komodo dragon (*Varanus komodoensis*)

KOMODO DRAGON
Varanus komodoensis

Physical characteristics: A thick-bodied animal, the Komodo dragon is the world's heaviest lizard. It can reach a weight of 330 pounds (150 kilograms) and a length up to 9.9 feet (3 meters) from snout to tail tip.

Geographic range: They live on a few Indonesian islands, including Komodo.

Habitat: Komodo dragons can live in dry or moist habitats and are good enough swimmers to spend some time in the water.

Diet: They are meat eaters, dining on deer, pigs, other mammals, lizards, and birds. The juvenile diet includes insects, bird and turtle eggs, and carrion.

The Komodo dragon is the world's heaviest lizard. It can reach a weight of 330 pounds (150 kilograms) (Erwin & Peggy Bauer/Bruce Coleman Inc. Reproduced by permission.)

Behavior and reproduction: Komodo dragons are active during the day, when they do their hunting. They either walk around looking for food or hunt by ambush. Juveniles are good climbers, but adults are too large to climb and stay on the ground. The mating season runs from May to August. In September, the females begin laying their eggs in burrows. The average nest contains about eighteen eggs, but some females can lay as many as three dozen at a time. The young hatch in March and April. When they reach eight or nine years old, they are ready to mate and become parents themselves.

Komodo dragons and people: Most people know of Komodo dragons from the zoo. Humans may find use for these lizards, because their blood contains special substances, called antibodies (AN-tee-BA-dees), that may someday help fight health problems in people.

Conservation status: Because the number of Komodo dragons is small, and they live in a very small area where their habitat is disappearing, the World Conservation Union (IUCN) considers these lizards to be Vulnerable, which means that they face a high risk of extinction in the wild. The U.S. Fish and Wildlife Service considers the lizards to be Endangered, which means that they are in danger of extinction throughout all or a significant portion of their range. ∎

Crocodile monitor (*Varanus salvadorii*)

CROCODILE MONITOR
Varanus salvadorii

Physical characteristics: The crocodile monitor is a long-tailed, yellow-spotted lizard that may grow to 12 feet (nearly 3.7 meters) in length from snout to tail tip, although some claim that the lizards may reach 15 to 19 feet (4.6 to 5.8 meters) long. It is often considered to be the world's longest lizard.

Geographic range: This lizard lives on southern New Guinea.

Habitat: The crocodile monitor frequently climbs into trees of the rainforest.

Diet: They probably eat birds in the wild, but in captivity, they also eat mice and rats.

The crocodile monitor is reported to be the world's longest lizard. They can grow to a length of 12 feet (nearly 3.7 meters). (©Tom McHugh/Photo Researchers, Inc. Reproduced by permission.)

Behavior and reproduction: Crocodile monitors spend much of their time in trees where they look for food. When they feel threatened, they will swing their tails like whips to strike an attacker. During mating season, the males wrestle one another. Females lay eggs, which hatch into large babies that can be 20 inches (0.5 meter) in length.

Crocodile monitors and people: Legends among the native people of New Guinea claim that this lizard is an evil spirit that breathes fire and eats men.

Conservation status: The crocodile monitor is not considered endangered or threatened. ■

FOR MORE INFORMATION

Books

Auffenberg, W. *The Behavioral Ecology of the Komodo Monitor*. Gainesville: University Press of Florida, 1981.

—— *The Bengal Monitor*. Gainesville: University Press of Florida, 1994.

—— *Gray's Monitor Lizard*. Gainesville: University Press of Florida, 1988.

Badger, D. *Lizards: A Natural History of Some Uncommon Creatures—Extraordinary Chameleons, Iguanas, Geckos, and More*. Stillwater, MN: Voyageur Press, 2002.

Bennett, D. *Monitor Lizards. Natural History, Biology and Husbandry*. Frankfurt am Main: Edition Chimaira, 1998.

King, D., and B. Green. *Goannas: The Biology of Varanid Lizards.* University of New South Wales Press, 1999.

Murphy, J. B., C. Ciofi, C. de la Panouse, and T. Walsh, eds. *Komodo Dragons: Biology and Conservation.* Washington, DC: Smithsonian Institution Press, 2002.

Pianka, E. R., and L. J. Vitt. *Lizards: Windows to the Evolution of Diversity.* Berkeley: University of California Press, 2003.

Periodicals

Mealy, Nora Steiner. "Creatures from Komodo." *Ranger Rick* (August 2001): http://www.findarticles.com/p/articles/mi_m0EPG/is_8_35/ ai_76289139 (accessed on October 18, 2004).

Web sites

"Crocodile Monitor." Honolulu Zoo. http://www.honoluluzoo.org/Crocodile_Monitor.htm (accessed on October 18, 2004).

"Komodo Dragon." Enchanted Learning. http://www.enchantedlearning .com/subjects/reptiles/lizard/Komodoprintout.shtml (accessed on October 18, 2004).

"Komodo Dragon." Honolulu Zoo. http://www.honoluluzoo.org/komodo_dragon.htm (accessed on October 18, 2004).

"Komodo Dragon, *Varanus komodoensis*, 1998." San Diego Zoo. http://library.sandiegozoo.org/Fact%20Sheets/komodo_dragon/Komodo.htm (accessed on October 18, 2004).

"New Guinea Crocodile Monitor." Central Florida Zoo. http://www .centralfloridazoo.org/animals/New_guinea_crocodile_monitor.htm (accessed on October 18, 2004).

"*Varanus komodoensis.*" Animal Diversity Web. http://animaldiversity .ummz.umich.edu/site/accounts/information/Varanus_komodoensis .html (accessed on October 18, 2004).

"Varanidae." Animal Diversity Web. http://animaldiversity.ummz.umich .edu/site/accounts/information/Varanida.html (accessed on October 18, 2004).

Class: Reptilia

Order: Squamata

Suborder: Serpentes

Family: Anomalepididae

Number of species: 16 species

CHAPTER

PHYSICAL CHARACTERISTICS

Early blind snakes are small, thin snakes, with many species reaching just 6 to 10 inches (15 to 25 centimeters) in length and less than one-tenth of an ounce (2.8 grams) in weight when full-grown. Five of the sixteen species are a bit larger and can top 12 inches (31 centimeters) in length, with some reaching as much as 16 inches (41 centimeters). The larger species include the greater blind snake and the four lesser blind snakes known by their scientific names. Most members of this family Anomalepididae have no common names and are known only by their scientific names. The typical early blind snake has a dark brown or black body with white, yellow, or pink on the head and tail. A few species lack the lighter color on the head and tail and are all reddish brown to brown.

The snakes in this family all have short heads with rounded snouts, and most have slightly larger scales on the snout than on the rest of the body. Compared to other snakes, their tongues are quite short. They have stumpy tails that make up just 1 to 3.4 percent of the snake's total body length. In snakes, the tail begins at the vent, a slitlike opening on the belly side of the animal. The tail in half of the early blind snake species is tipped with a thin, sharp spine. The other species have tails without spines.

They look much like slender blind snakes of the family Leptotyphlopidae and blind snakes of the family Typhlopidae. The snakes in all three families have tube-shaped bodies that are covered in smooth, round scales. Unlike most snakes that have belly scales, or ventrals, that are noticeably larger than the scales on the sides and back, the members of these three families have belly scales that are about the same size as the others. The three families also share a few other traits. All have small mouths that open not on the front end of the head as in most other snakes, but slightly before the front end and on the bottom. They have tiny eyes that are barely noticeable, if they are noticeable at all, beneath scales on the head.

Early blind snakes do have some differences from the other two blind snake families. Early blind snakes have teeth on both the upper and lower jaws, while snakes in the other families have them only on the upper jaw or only on the lower jaw. In addition, early blind snakes have more scale rows than the others. Scientists determine scale rows by counting the number of scales from the belly up the side over the top and down the other side. Most early blind snakes have more than 20 scale rows.

Early blind snakes sometimes go by the common names of primitive or dawn blind snakes. Because many individuals have a head and tail that are very hard to tell apart, they are also sometimes called two-headed snakes.

TANGLED FAMILIES

Although some sources lump the blind snakes together in one family, most scientists place them in three separate families: the blind snakes of the family Typhlopidae, the early blind snakes of the family Anomalepididae, and the slender blind snakes of the family Leptotyphlopidae. The early blind snakes first got their own family in 1939 when Edward H. Taylor noticed several differences in them from other blind snakes, including a greater number of scale rows and the presence of teeth on both jaws instead of just one or the other. They also have an unusually shaped bone, called the hyoid (HIGH-oid), that supports the tongue. In early blind snakes, it is M-shaped, rather than the typical V- or Y-shape seen in other snakes.

GEOGRAPHIC RANGE

Early blind snakes live in southern Central America, across northern South America and possibly on Trinidad, and then down the eastern side of South America to northeastern Argentina. Of the four main groups, or genera (jen-AIR-uh), in this family, two live from Costa Rica to northern South America. These include the four species in the genus (JEAN-us) (the singular of genera) *Anomalepis* and the three species in the genus *Helminthophis*. The two species of the genus *Typhlophis* live only in South America, from central Venezuela eastward through French Guiana and southward through northeastern Brazil. One species may extend onto Trinidad. The largest genus is *Liotyphlops* with eight species. Some of these live from Costa Rica into northern South America, and others make their homes farther south in southern Brazil, southeastern Paraguay, and northeastern Argentina.

One species, *Helminthophis flavoterminatus*, lives on the Indian Ocean island of Mauritius, far away from the other early blind snakes. Humans are likely responsible for bringing the snake to the island.

HABITAT

These snakes live most of their lives below the ground; one individual was reported buried 1.6 feet (0.5 meters) deep in the soil. They also spend time beneath rocks, logs, and piles of leaves. Like other underground-living, or fossorial (faw-SOR-ee-ul), species that stay out of human sight and live in remote areas, scientists know little about them. People have reported these snakes in a number of different habitats from dry forests to rainforests, and from low-lying grasslands to nearly 6,000 feet (1,830 meters) up rocky mountainsides. Although no one has seen early blind snakes doing it, scientists suspect that they can and do climb trees.

DIET

At least two species eat ant eggs, as well as ant larvae (LAR-vee) and pupae (PEW-pee), which are the life stages between the egg and the adult ant. Scientists suspect that other early blind snakes also eat ants and possibly other insects, but they have not studied them in enough detail to say for sure.

BEHAVIOR AND REPRODUCTION

Scientists know little about their behavior in the wild but suspect that they remain active all year and mainly at night. In captivity, the snakes stay underground most of the time. When picked up by a person, an early blind snake defends itself by squirming and twisting its body and then releasing body waste —both of which may cause the person to lose grip or let go of the snake. If it has a spine-tipped tail, the snake will also jab it into the person's hand.

Snake researchers guess that the early blind snakes probably lay eggs rather than give birth to live babies, but they have not studied them enough to be sure. No information is available on when or how the snakes mate or on how many young they have.

EARLY BLIND SNAKES AND PEOPLE

Early blind snakes and people rarely encounter one another.

CONSERVATION STATUS

These species are not listed as endangered or threatened. Like many other species that live much of their lives underground, however, scientists have little information about their numbers in the wild. In fact, scientists know about six of the sixteen species only from a few individuals caught in the area where the first ones were found, and they have not seen one species, the South American blind snake (*Anomalepis aspinosus*), since 1916.

Lesser blind snake (*Liotyphlops ternetzii*)

SPECIES ACCOUNT

LESSER BLIND SNAKE
Liotyphlops ternetzii

Physical characteristics: One of the larger members of the family, lesser blind snake adults can grow to more than 12 inches (31 centimeters) in length. It is a thin, black, wormlike snake with white on its head. Its shiny body is covered with small scales that are all about the same size. It has tiny eyes and a small mouth that opens on the bottom of the head rather than in front like the mouths in most other snakes. Its body is tube-shaped and ends with a short spine-tipped tail. Its skeleton includes bits of hip bones that are leftover reminders of its ancient ancestors, which had legs.

Geographic range: The lesser blind snake lives in Central and South America.

Habitat: This species spends most of its time underground, beneath rocks or logs, or in other hiding places.

Diet: They eat ant eggs, larvae, and pupae. The larvae and pupae are the life stages between the egg and the adult ant. They may also eat other insects.

Behavior and reproduction: Scientists know almost nothing about their behavior and reproduction. They suspect, however, that these snakes are active at night throughout the year and that they lay eggs.

Lesser blind snakes and people: Lesser blind snakes and people rarely encounter one another.

Conservation status: The species is not listed as endangered or threatened, but scientists have little information about their numbers in the wild. ■

One of the larger members of the family, lesser blind snake adults can grow to more than 12 inches (31 centimeters) in length. (Illustration by Emily Damstra. Reproduced by permission.)

FOR MORE INFORMATION

Books

Brazaitis, P., and M. Watanabe. *Snakes of the World.* New York: Crescent Books, 1992.

Greene, Harry W. *Snakes: The Evolution of Mystery in Nature.* Berkeley: University of California Press, 1997.

McDiarmid, Roy W., Jonathan A. Campbell, and T'Shaka A. Touré. *Snake Species of the World: A Taxonomic and Geographic Reference.* Vol. 1. Washington, DC: Herpetologists' League, 1999.

Mehrtens, John M. *Living Snakes of the World in Color.* New York: Sterling Publishing. 1987.

Peters, James A., and Braulio R. Orejas-Miranda. *Catalogue of the Neotropical Squamata.* Vol. 1, *Snakes.* Washington, DC: Smithsonian Institution Press, 1970.

Taylor, Barbara. *Snakes.* New York: Lorenz: 1998.

Web sites

"Blind snake (Typhlopidae)." MavicaNET. http://www.mavicanet.ru/directory/eng/24710.html (accessed on October 5, 2004).

"Blindsnakes (Infraorder Scolecophidia)." Singapore Zoological Gardens. http://www.szgdocent.org/cc/c-blind.htm (accessed on September 29, 2004).

"Family Anomalepidae (Dawn Blind Snakes)." EMBL Reptile Database. http://www.embl-heidelberg.de/uetz/families/Anomalepidae.html (accessed on October 5, 2004).

"Superfamiliy Typhlopoidea (blind snakes)." The University of Michigan Museum of Zoology, Animal Diversity Web. http://animaldiversity.ummz.umich.edu/site/accounts/pictures/Typhlopoidea.html (accessed on October 5, 2004).

CHAPTER

PHYSICAL CHARACTERISTICS

Slender blind snakes, which are also known as thread snakes or worm snakes, are thin snakes with smooth, shiny scales. Members of this family look much like blind snakes of the family Typhlopidae and the early blind snakes of the family Anomalepididae, since all have tube-shaped bodies that are about the same diameter from head to tail, and all have short heads with mouths that open downward instead of right on the front end of the head. Species within the three blind snake families have small eyes and bodies that are covered with small scales that are the same size on the belly as they are on the sides and back. In most snakes, the belly scales, or ventrals, are noticeably larger. In the three blind snake families, only the scales on the snout are larger.

The slender blind snakes are different from the other two families in several ways. While all are slim, the slender blind snakes are the thinnest. The bodies of most species within this family are no wider than 0.2 inches (0.5 centimeters), and some are as little as 1/25th of an inch (1 millimeter) wide. This gives them the appearance of moving string or thread. The largest species in the family, such as the western slender blind snake (also known as the southwestern thread snake) and the western thread snake, may reach more than 15 inches (38 centimeters) in length, but most of the 93 species in the family are much smaller. The typical adult ranges from 4 to 10 inches (10 to 25 centimeters) in length and no more than 0.05 ounces (1.4 grams) in weight. Another characteristic that sets the slender blind snakes apart from the other blind snakes—and indeed

phylum

class

subclass

order

monotypic order

suborder

▲ **family**

Class: Reptilia

Order: Squamata

Suborder: Serpentes

Family: Typhlopidae

Number of species: 214 species

family

CHAPTER

phylum

class

subclass

order

monotypic order

suborder

▲ **family**

PHYSICAL CHARACTERISTICS

Most blind snakes are small, with many species reaching less than 12 inches (31 centimeters) in length at full size. Adult flowerpot snakes, for example, reach only 4 to 6.5 inches (10 to 16.5 centimeters) long. A few species, however, can grow to more than 24 inches (61 centimeters). The largest, known as Peter's giant blind snake or the Zambezi blind snake, can top 3 feet (0.9 meters) in length and weigh 1.1 pounds (0.5 kilograms).

The typical blind snake is smooth and shiny with a tube-shaped body. Usually, the head, body, and tail have about the same diameter, although in a few of the larger species, the back half of the animal may grow fat and become quite thick. The scales on their backs are thick and noticeably overlap one another. In some other families of snakes, the scales barely overlap, if they overlap at all. Such an arrangement of overlapping, thick scales gives the blind snakes a strong protective cover.

Blind snakes have short heads, typically with small eyes covered by a see-through scale and a small mouth that opens on the underside of the snake rather than on the front of the head like most other snakes. In some species, the snout is rounded, but in others it may flatten out toward the front, become pointed or hooked, or have some other shape. A few species have little bits of flesh that stick out of the front of the snout and are used by the snake to feel its way along the dark, underground tunnels in which it lives. The tails are usually rather short and often tipped with a single, thorny spine. The spine is especially noticeable in *Typhlops depressiceps* and *Acutotyphlops subocularis*. The tail in a snake begins at the vent, a slitlike opening on the snake's underside. They range from tails that make up less than 1/100th of the body length to tails in some species that consist of 1/10th of the overall body.

Many blind snakes have brown, dark gray, or black backs, and a few have bright patterns, such as speckles, blotches, or stripes of white, yellow, orange, or blue. The bellies are often a lighter color than the backs. A few of the blind snakes, including the *Xenotyphlops grandidieri*, are completely uncolored and look a rather sickly white.

GEOGRAPHIC RANGE

Blind snakes are found in tropical areas nearly around the world, including New Guinea and Australia, Southeast Asia, Africa and Madagascar, the Middle East, southeastern Europe, Mexico, Central America, and northern South America. They are also found on many islands in the Pacific and Indian oceans and in the West Indies. One species, commonly called the flowerpot blind snake or Brahminy blind snake, has traveled throughout the world, including the United States, in plant shipments. Many people mistake this species for an earthworm, but the snake is shiny, has a light-colored underside, and lacks the rings around its body that worms have.

HABITAT

Blind snakes are burrowing species that spend most of their lives either underground or out of sight under logs, tree bark, stones, or in some other hiding place. Some will even slither into ant or termite hills. Rainy weather seems to persuade many blind snakes to leave their underground homes and crawl out onto land. A few species have been found in trees, but they may not actually live there and instead be just visiting to look for a meal. Some blind snakes live in wet rainforests, but other species survive quite well in deserts. Many others live in grasslands, dry forests, farm fields, sandy beaches at the oceanside, or high up mountainsides. Almost half of the species are found only on islands, and about 85 percent of all species of blind snakes live only in the Old World, which includes Asia, Europe, and Africa in the Eastern Hemisphere.

DIET

Blind snakes eat termites, ants, worms, and other small invertebrates (in-VER-teh-brehts). Invertebrates are animals

NOT THE WHOLE SKIN

Snakes do not shed all of their skin. Instead, they shed only the outermost layer, called the stratum corneum (STRAT-um kor-NEE-um). When a snake sheds, or molts, the stratum corneum comes loose, and the snake slips out of it so that it peels off and leaves a complete, inside-out shed that is thin and nearly see-through. In the blind snake of the family Typhlopidae, which has an exceptionally thick stratum corneum, the shed comes off not in an entire piece but in bits and pieces that look like a number of rubbery rings.

without backbones. Some of the insects attempt to bite or sting in defense, but the thick, overlapping scales on the blind snake protect it from harm. The snakes follow ant trails to their nests by flicking out their tongues, which they use to smell and taste the trail. They are very fast eaters, sometimes gobbling up to 100 insects in just a minute's time. They can eat so rapidly because their upper teeth can be pushed out and then pulled back into the mouth, somewhat like a fast-moving rake. When they find an anthill, for example, they can rake through it and pull in prey very quickly.

BEHAVIOR AND REPRODUCTION

As is true with many other burrowing species that remain out of sight most of the time, scientists know little about their behavior or reproduction. When they are dug out of their burrows, the snakes quickly try to bury themselves again. If they are captured, they will wiggle wildly, ooze a bad-smelling material from the vent area, release their body waste, and/or poke the tail spine into the attacker. Any of these actions can cause the attacker to drop the snake. Occasionally, up to twenty individuals from some species of blind snakes coil up together under a stone. Scientists are unsure why they do it, but they think the snakes are just sharing a good spot.

Most blind snakes lay eggs, but in a few species, the eggs may hatch inside the mother so that she gives birth to live baby snakes. The flowerpot snake may be parthenogenetic (PAR-thih-no-jeh-NEH-tik), which means that the females do not need males to fertilize their eggs in order to have babies. It is the only parthenogenetic snake, and one of the few parthenogenetic vertebrates in the entire animal kingdom. Vertebrates (VER-teh-brehts) are animals with backbones. Among blind snakes overall, small or especially thin species have fewer eggs — sometimes just one, raisin-sized egg. Larger species may have more than fifty eggs that are the size of large grapes. Eggs probably hatch in one to two months, but some hatch in just a week. Many of the blind snakes mate during only one season a year, usually in late spring, but others appear to mate all year long.

BLIND SNAKES AND PEOPLE

Many African and Asian cultures mention blind snakes in their legends and folklore.

CONSERVATION STATUS

The World Conservation Union (IUCN) lists the Mona Island blind snake as Endangered, which means it faces a very high risk of extinction in the wild. It also lists the Christmas Island blind snake as Vulnerable, which means it faces a high risk of extinction in the wild. Scientists know little about the wild populations of many species, however, so others may be at risk.

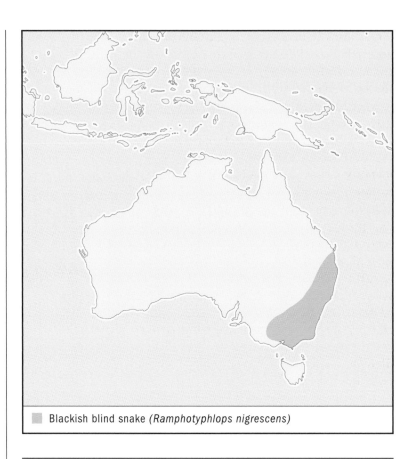

Blackish blind snake (*Ramphotyphlops nigrescens*)

BLACKISH BLIND SNAKE
Ramphotyphlops nigrescens

Physical characteristics: The blackish blind snake, also known as the English blind snake, has a dark back and lighter belly. The back may be black, purple, or pinkish brown, while the underside is pink or off-white. The vent may have a dark blotch on either side. The snout is short and rounded. Size ranges from 3.8 to 22.7 inches (9.7 to 57.6 centimeters) long, and the females are much larger than the males.

Geographic range: Blackish blind snakes live in the eastern half of Australia.

Habitat: People usually see these snakes while turning over rocks or other items in gardens, farm fields, or even in city lots. The snakes also live in similar hiding spots in the woods and along the coastline.

Diet: Blackish blind snakes eat ant larvae (LAR-vee) and pupae (PYU-pee), which are the stages in an ant's life between egg and juvenile. They will also eat worms and other small invertebrates once in a while. A single blackish blind snake can eat 1,500 ants or more at one sitting. The snakes usually only feed in the spring and summer.

Behavior and reproduction: Blackish blind snakes are a burrowing species that spends much of its time underground. Up to thirty members of the species sometimes group together to share a good spot under a stone or in some other hiding spot. After a heavy rain, blackish blind snakes may leave their burrows and slither about on the ground, sometimes even climbing into trees. This species mates in late spring, and the females lay five to twenty grape-sized eggs at a time in the summer.

A single blackish blind snake can eat 1,500 ants or more at one sitting. (Illustration by Bruce Worden. Reproduced by permission.)

Blackish blind snakes and people: People and these snakes generally leave one another alone.

Conservation status: The species is not listed as endangered or threatened. ■

FOR MORE INFORMATION

Books

Burnie, David, and Don Wilson, eds. *The Definitive Visual Guide to the World's Wildlife.* New York: DK Publishing, 2001.

Cogger, H. G. *Reptiles and Amphibians of Australia.* Fifth ed. Ithaca, NY: Comstock Publishing Associates/Cornell University Press, 1994.

Ehmann, H., and M. J. Bamford. "Family Typhlopidae." In *Fauna of Australia.* Vol. 2A, *Amphibia & Reptilia,* edited by C. J. Glasby, G. J. B. Ross, and P. L. Beesley. Canberra: Australian Government Publishing Service, 1993.

FitzSimons, V. F. M. *Snakes of Southern Africa.* Cape Town and Johannesburg: Purnell and Sons, 1962.

Grace, Eric, ed. *Snakes.* San Francisco: Sierra Club Books for Children, 1994.

Greer, A. E. *The Biology and Evolution of Australian Snakes.* Chipping Norton, New South Wales, Australia: Surrey Beatty & Sons, 1997.

Lee, Alfonso Silva. *Coquí y sus amigos / Coquí and His Friends.* Pangaea, Bilingual edition, 2000.

McDiarmid, R. W., J. A. Campbell, and T. A. Touré. *Snake Species of the World: A Taxonomic and Geographic Reference.* Vol. 1. Washington, DC: Herpetologists' League, 1999.

Mehrtens, John M. *Living Snakes of the World in Color.* New York: Sterling Publishing, 1987.

Schwartz, A., and R. W. Henderson. *Amphibians and Reptiles of the West Indies: Descriptions, Distributions, and Natural History.* Gainesville: University of Florida Press, 1991.

Taylor, Barbara. *Snakes.* New York: Lorenz, 1998.

Web sites

"Blindsnake." Wild Kids. http://www.amonline.net.au/wild_kids/reptiles/ blind_snake.htm (accessed on September 22, 2004).

"Blind Snakes, Family Typhlopidae." Australian Museum. http://www .livingharbour.net/reptiles/snakes_blind.htm (accessed on September 22, 2004).

"Blind Snakes (Family Typhlopidae: South-east Queensland." Queensland Museum Explorer. http://www.qmuseum.qld.gov.au/features/snakes/ seq/typhlopidae.asp (accessed on September 23, 2004).

"Brahminy Blind Snake." Ohio Public Library Information Network. http://www.oplin.org/snake/fact%20pages/brahminy_blind/brahminy .html (accessed on September 22, 2004).

FALSE BLIND SNAKES

Anomochilidae

Class: Reptilia

Order: Squamata

Suborder: Serpentes

Family: Anomochilidae

Number of species: 2 species

PHYSICAL CHARACTERISTICS

False blind snakes are also known as dwarf pipe snakes because, at first glance, they look very much like small pipe snakes. Pipe snakes actually fall under a separate family, the Cylindrophiidae. The false blind snake has a short head and a short tail on either end of a tube-shaped body. In snakes, the tail is the portion of the body that begins at the vent, a crosswise opening on the belly side and toward the rear of a snake. On either side of the vent, these snakes have a tiny bit of bone that sticks out. These bones are called spurs and are seen in a few other snake families, including the boas.

Their backs are a dark reddish color blotched with yellowish white markings. The eyes and mouth in a false blind snake are small. In most snakes, the mouth opens at the very tip of the head, but in false blind snakes, it opens slightly before the end of the head. Both species in this family have seventeen to nineteen scale rows. In other words, if a person counted the number of scales in a straight line from the belly over the back the snake and back down to the belly, he or she would find seventeen to nineteen rows. The number of scales on the underside of the snake from front to back is between 222 and 252 in the false blind snake known as *Anomochilus leonardi* and between 236 and 248 in the snake *Anomochilus weberi*. The common name for both species is false blind snake. The short tail in both species only has six to eight scales on the underside.

Based on the specimens in museums, adult false blind snakes range from 8 to 14 inches (20 to 36 centimeters) in length.

phylum

class

subclass

order

monotypic order

suborder

▲ **family**

Scientists have studied only museum specimens rather than living snakes in the wild.

GEOGRAPHIC RANGE

False blind snakes are found in Borneo, the Malaysian Peninsula, and Sumatra.

HABITAT

False blind snakes probably live in loose soil or under leaves, but this is uncertain. Only a few individuals have been found, and these have been spread out in such a way that some scientists now think that the two species are really just different populations of one species, while others believe that the snakes should be split into more than two species.

DIET

False blind snakes probably eat worms and insect larvae (LAR-vee), which may include grubs or caterpillars, but this is just a guess. No one has studied a live false blind snake. In addition, no researcher has found a dead one and opened up its stomach to see what it had been eating.

BEHAVIOR AND REPRODUCTION

Scientists have never studied a live false blind snake, so they know nothing about its behavior. They did, however, find one female that had shelled eggs still inside her. From this, they guessed that the species lays eggs. Snakes, however, fall into three groups. One of them is oviparous (oh-VIH-puh-rus), which means that the female produces and lays shelled eggs. The babies in the eggs get all their necessary food from inside the egg until they hatch. The second group is viviparous (vie-VIH-puh-rus), which means that the mother makes no eggs, provides all of the food for the babies through connections inside of her body, and gives birth to baby snakes. No eggs are involved. The third group is ovoviviparous (oh-voh-vie-VIH-puh-rus), which falls somewhere between oviparous and viviparous. The females in ovoviviparous species produce eggs, but the eggs hatch inside her body just before she gives birth. The babies, then, get food from the egg rather than directly from the

MYSTERIES BELOW

As humans build ships to travel to space or deep in the oceans, a wide variety of life forms go unnoticed beneath our feet. Many of the species that spend their lives out of view in underground tunnels or even just underneath piles of leaves are overlooked. The false blind snakes are a good example. Although they live over a large region in Indonesia, scientists have only found a few and have never studied a living specimen. The same holds true for many other underground species, which leaves wide open a huge area of study for future biologists.

mother, but are born as baby snakes. Only oviparous species are considered to be egg-layers. The other two groups are said to be live-bearing snakes, meaning that they give birth to baby snakes rather than eggs. Since scientists have only seen eggs in a dead female but have never seen one give birth, they cannot tell for sure whether this species is oviparous or ovoviviparous.

FALSE BLIND SNAKES AND PEOPLE

False blind snakes continue to live their lives outside the view of people.

CONSERVATION STATUS

The World Conservation Union (IUCN) considers the two false blind snakes to be Data Deficient, which means that scientists as yet have too little information to make a judgment about the threat of extinction.

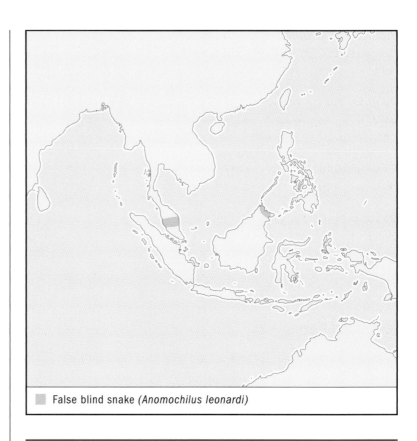
False blind snake *(Anomochilus leonardi)*

FALSE BLIND SNAKE
Anomochilus leonardi

Physical characteristics: The false blind snake has a tube-shaped body, a short head with small eyes and mouth, and a short tail. At first glance, it is difficult to tell which end is the head and which is the tail. It has small, oblong, whitish spots down its dark red to brown back. Adults range from 8 to 14 inches (20 to 36 centimeters) in length. The size range may change a bit once scientists study more false blind snakes.

Geographic range: False blind snakes live in the Malaysian Peninsula and Borneo.

Habitat: They probably live in loose soil or under leaves, but this is uncertain.

Diet: They probably eat invertebrates, which are insects, worms, and other animals without backbones.

Behavior and reproduction: False blind snakes are probably egg-layers, although this in uncertain. Their behavior and reproduction are unknown.

False blind snakes and people: People see this snake only very rarely and generally leave it alone.

Conservation status: The World Conservation Union (IUCN) considers the false blind snake to be Data Deficient, which means that scientists as yet have too little information to make a judgment about the threat of extinction. ■

False blind snakes are found in Borneo, the Malaysian Peninsula, and Sumatra. (Illustration by Emily Damstra. Reproduced by permission.)

FOR MORE INFORMATION

Books

David, P., and G. Vogel. *The Snakes of Sumatra.* Frankfurt am Main, Germany: Edition Chimaira, 1996.

Greene, H. W. *Snakes: The Evolution of Mystery in Nature.* Berkeley: University of California Press, 1999.

Mehrtens, John M. *Living Snakes of the World in Color.* New York: Sterling Publishing, 1987.

Web sites

"Family Anomochilidae (Dwarf Pipe Snakes)." Animal Diversity Web. http://animaldiversity.ummz.umich.edu/site/accounts/information/Anomochilidae.html (accessed on September 21, 2004).

"Pipe Snakes and Shield Snakes." Singapore Zoological Gardens. http://www.szgdocent.org/cc/c-pipe.htm (accessed on September 22, 2004).

PHYSICAL CHARACTERISTICS

Almost all of the forty-seven species of shieldtail snakes have a head that gets narrower and narrower until it comes to a point at the end. In some species, the head gets narrower from side to side, and in others it narrows from top to bottom. The pointed snout is covered with thick scales made of fingernail-like material, and in some snakes, a particularly large scale makes a roof over the top of the snout. Many species have a large scale at the very end of the tail. This large scale looks something like a shield, which is how the snakes got their common name of shieldtails. The large tail scale may have ridges, or keels, or it may be covered with spines. Often, the snake has other thick and keeled scales that form a flattened oval just in front of the shield scale. If the snakes live in wet areas, these keels and spines can pick up and hold mud, which may form into a large clump.

Many species are brown, gray, or black. Some have dark bands. A number of species have white or yellowish white outlines around their belly scales, which can make them look rather speckled. Some shieldtails have bright yellow bellies marked with dark spots, and blue, so-called iridescent (IH-rih-DEH-sent) backs that shimmer different colors when the light strikes them. A few species in Sri Lanka look like members of the cobra family. This type of copying, called mimicry (pronounced MIM-ick-ree), actually causes some birds that might otherwise attack the snakes to stay away.

Although it cannot be seen from the outside, shieldtail snakes are different from other snakes in the kind of muscle tissue that they have in the trunk, or portion of the body between the head and the tail. In snakes, the tail begins at the vent, a slitlike opening on the underside of the snake. The muscles in the front part of the trunk in shieldtails have red muscle fibers in addition to the white muscle fibers present in other snakes. The red fibers can work longer than the white ones without tiring out, and scientists believe that these long-lasting fibers help the snake, which spends much of its time digging.

Shieldtail snakes are mostly small snakes, with most adults growing to less than 12 inches (30 centimeters) in length. Some grow longer, and a few such as the *Rhinophis oxyrhynchus* and *Uropeltis ocellatus* can reach nearly 24 inches (61 centimeters) in length.

GEOGRAPHIC RANGE

Shieldtail snakes live in southern India and in Sri Lanka or Ceylon, which is located off India's southern coast.

HABITAT

Shieldtail snakes make their homes in forests that may be in low areas or on the sides of mountains, usually preferring places with moist or wet ground. They also live in gardens and farm fields, including rubber plantations. Unlike most digging snakes that only push through loose soil, the shieldtails will also tunnel through quite hard, clay soils. In addition, they will scoot under leaves or logs.

DIET

Shieldtails mainly eat worms, but some species will also eat caterpillars and termites, and at least one species in captivity will eat earwigs. Earwigs are small insects with a pair of pincers on the end of the body. After studying how several species eat worms, scientists found that the snakes either grab the worm at the end or in the middle and quickly drag them back into the burrow. The bodies of those worms caught in the middle fold in half as they are dragged into the snake's narrow burrow.

BURROWING BY JERKS

Some scientists believe that the shieldtail snakes burrow through the ground with an odd jerking movement. According to this idea, the snakes twist up the backbone behind the head so that it is curved back and forth and then quickly push the backbone out straight to burst the head forward. In other words, the back acts like a spring that is squeezed together and then let loose. By repeating this movement and scooting up the body each time, the snake digs through the soil. This is the same type of jerking movement used by pipe snakes, but pipe snakes use it to force the head forward as a way of gulping down large prey.

BEHAVIOR AND REPRODUCTION

The shieldtails stay hidden underground most of the time, but many will come up to the surface after a good rain, and at least one species will then begin hunting for worms. If the snakes feel threatened, they will wiggle away while looking for some loose soil and then force the head into the ground to start tunneling. They are expert diggers and can tunnel quickly. If prodded with a stick or otherwise attacked, the snake will coil around the stick or other object and begin waving the tail end of the body. Apparently, predators are confused into thinking the tail is the head. The snake can survive an attack to the tail much better than an attack to the head, so the tail waving may save its life. It is also possible that some predators may be scared off by the tail-waving behavior.

Female shieldtail snakes give birth to baby snakes rather than laying eggs. Typically, they have two to five young at a time, with larger females giving birth to a larger number than younger mothers. Births likely occur between March and September. Scientists know little else about their behavior or reproduction.

SHIELDTAIL SNAKES AND PEOPLE

These snakes and people rarely encounter each other.

CONSERVATION STATUS

These species are not listed as endangered or threatened, but scientists know little about the size of the snakes' populations.

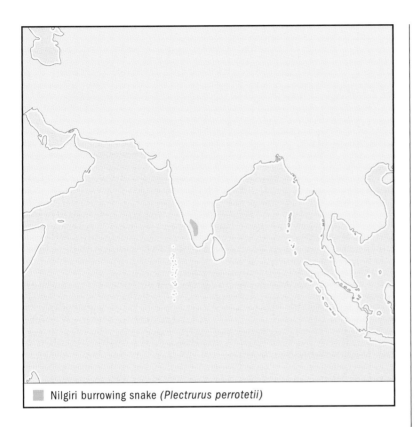

Nilgiri burrowing snake (*Plectrurus perrotetii*)

NILGIRI BURROWING SNAKE
Plectrurus perrotetii

Physical characteristics: One of the larger species in this family, the Nilgiri burrowing snake can reach 17.3 inches (44 centimeters) in length. They are tube-shaped snakes with purplish brown to brown backs and bellies that are often either a light brown or yellowish color. In some species, the bellies are spotted with a lighter color, and each of these spots is located right in the center of a belly scale. The head is flattened from top to bottom. The tail is tipped with a spiny, cup-shaped scale.

Geographic range: The snake lives in Nilgiri and the Anamalai Hills in southern India.

Habitat: Most of the snakes found by people are buried about 4 to 6 inches (10 to 15 centimeters) deep in the very rich soil of gardens

or farm fields. The snakes especially like soil with lots of manure mixed into it. Farmers and gardeners often use manure, which contains many nutrients, to fertilize their soil and help their plants to grow. The snakes live high up on hillsides.

Diet: The Nilgiri burrowing snake eats mainly worms.

Behavior and reproduction: They spend much of their time in burrows, but if the weather turns cooler, they will move out of their homes and explore piles of manure that farmers and gardeners have left above the ground. They give birth to baby snakes rather than laying eggs. Females have three to six babies at a time, usually in July or August. Scientists know little else about their behavior or reproduction.

One of the larger species in this family, the Nilgiri burrowing snake can reach 17.3 inches (44 centimeters) in length. (Illustration by Bruce Worden. Reproduced by permission.)

Nilgiri burrowing snakes and people: These snakes and people rarely see or bother each other.

Conservation status: The Nilgiri burrowing snake is not listed as endangered or threatened, but scientists know little about the size of the snake's population. ■

FOR MORE INFORMATION

Books

Burnie, David, and Don Wilson, eds. *The Definitive Visual Guide to the World's Wildlife.* New York: DK Publishing, 2001.

Deraniyagala, P. E. P. *A Colored Atlas of Some Vertebrates from Ceylon.* Vol. 3, *Serpentoid Reptilia.* Colombo, Sri Lanka: Government Press, 1955.

Frank, N., and E. Ramus. *A Complete Guide to Scientific and Common Names of Reptiles and Amphibians of the World.* Pottsville, PA: NG Publishing, 1996.

Grace, Eric, ed. *Snakes.* San Francisco: Sierra Club Books for Children, 1994.

McDiarmid, R. W., J. A. Campbell, and T. A. Toure. *Snake Species of the World*, Vol. 1. Washington, DC: The Herpetologists' League, 1999.

Mehrtens, John M. *Living Snakes of the World in Color.* New York: Sterling Publishing, 1987.

Pough, F. H., R. M. Andrews, J. E. Cadle, M. L. Crump, A. H. Savitzky, and K. D. Wells. *Herpetology*, 2nd ed. Upper Saddle River, NJ: Prentice Hall, 2001.

Rajendran, M. V. *Studies in Uropeltid Snakes.* Madurai, India: Madurai Kamaraj University Publications, 1985.

Smith, M. A. *The Fauna of British India, Ceylon and Burma, Including the Whole of the Indo-Chinese Sub-Region. Reptilia and Amphibia.* Vol. 3, *Serpentes.* London: Taylor and Francis, 1943.

Web sites

"Family Uropeltidae (shield-tailed snakes and short-tail snakes)." Animal Diversity Web. http://animaldiversity.ummz.umich.edu/site/accounts/pictures/Uropeltidae. html (accessed on September 22, 2004).

PIPE SNAKES
Cylindrophiidae

Class: Reptilia
Order: Squamata
Suborder: Serpentes
Family: Cylindrophiidae
Number of species: 9 species

phylum

class

subclass

order

monotypic order

suborder

▲ **family**

PHYSICAL CHARACTERISTICS

The family name Cylindrophiidae points out one of the pipe snakes' most noticeable features: their tube- or cylinder-shaped bodies. The family includes nine species, which are often called Asian pipe snakes to set them apart from other families of snakes that some people also call pipe snakes. These include the somewhat similar-looking false coral snakes of the family Aniliidae and the false blind snakes of the family Anomochilidae.

The pipe snakes are usually dark brown to black with yellow or reddish bands running from the belly up the sides of the back. The back bands are sometimes very pale and difficult to see. The underside of the tail, however, usually has a very bright red or yellow tip. Some pipe snakes have stripes, and others have light-colored spots that color the middle of the snake's back from head to tail. Counted from one side over the back and down the other side, they have seventeen to twenty-three rows of scales. The head, which is no wider than the neck, is rounded and contains two small eyes with round or slightly oblong pupils and two nostrils that each sit inside a single scale. Pipe snakes also have a very short, pointy tail that is about as thick as the rest of the body. The tail in a snake begins at the vent, a slitlike opening on the underside of the animal. Pipe snakes are small- to medium-sized snakes, ranging from 1 to 3 feet (0.4 to 1 meters) long.

GEOGRAPHIC RANGE

Pipe snakes live in Indonesia, including Borneo, Sumatra, and Aru Island west of New Guinea; Sri Lanka or Ceylon off the coast of southern India; and southern China. They also exist in much of Southeast Asia, including Thailand, Laos, Cambodia, Myanmar, and Vietnam.

HABITAT

Pipe snakes tend to live in low-lying forests near a water source and in rice paddies, but they may also crawl into nearby villages and towns. They often slither under leaves or into soft, moist soil on the ground. They are also excellent swimmers.

DIET

The red-tailed pipe snake, and probably the other eight species, eats long and thin animals, including other snakes, eels, and lengthy lizards. For this reason, their jaws do not need to open as wide and their necks and bodies do not need to stretch as much as other snakes, which eat prey that are larger around. The pipe snakes are constrictors (kun-STRIK-tuhrs), which means that the snake will grasp its prey by looping its body around the animal and squeezing. For small prey, the snake may hold the animal just until it can reach its head around and eat it. For larger animals, the snake squeezes the prey until it cannot breathe and stops moving before eating it. People who keep pipe snakes in captivity find that the snakes will also eat small mice and fish.

THE NAME GAME

Scientific names for animals, such as *Cylindrophis ruffus*, may appear to be long and confusing, but they actually make it much easier for researchers to tell animals apart. This is because all scientists around the world use the same scientific names no matter what language they speak. This is not true of common names. For example, among just the English-speaking people, some use the common name of pipe snake for the nine species in the family Cylindrophiidae, but others use it to mean the species in the family Aniliidae or those in the family Anomochilidae. A scientific name has two parts: the genus name, which notes the general group to which the animal belongs, and the species name, which reveals the exact type of animal. In addition, the genus name tells scientists which animals are the most closely related. All nine members of the Cylindrophiidae family, for instance, are of the same genus and are therefore closely related.

Pipe snakes swallow in an unusual way. After swallowing part-way with some of the prey still hanging outside, the snake shuts its mouth, curves its backbone back and forth, and then reopens its mouth while quickly straightening out the backbone, which causes the head to shoot forward over more of the prey's body. Some people believe the snake may dig through the soil by the same method, but no one has seen this.

BEHAVIOR AND REPRODUCTION

Pipe snakes stay out of sight in the dirt or under leaves much of the time but will crawl about above ground after a heavy rain.

The red-tailed pipe snake is mostly known for its behavior when it feels threatened. The snake will flatten out its body and raise its tail, moving it much as a cobra would wave its flattened neck and head. (Illustration by Bruce Worden. Reproduced by permission.)

Habitat: Red-tailed pipe snakes spend most of their time under leaves or in burrows that they can dig themselves. They live in forests, often near a water source, and in rice paddies, but they may also live in nearby villages and towns.

Diet: It eats other snakes, lizards, and eels. A constrictor, it is able to squeeze the prey animals until they cannot breathe and either pass out or die before being eaten.

Behavior and reproduction: The red-tailed pipe snake is mostly known for its behavior when it feels threatened. The snake will flatten out its body and raise its tail, moving it much as a cobra would wave its flattened neck and head. Although the tail can do no harm, the display is often enough to convince an attacking animal to leave the snake alone. This species gives birth to baby snakes rather than eggs. The females typically have two young at a time but occasionally have up to twelve. Young are about 7 inches (18 centimeters) long at birth.

Red-tailed pipe snakes and people: Humans and these snakes have little contact.

Conservation status: These species are not listed as endangered or threatened. Like many other species that live much of their lives underground, however, scientists have little information about their numbers in the wild.   ■

FOR MORE INFORMATION

Books

Burnie, David, and Don Wilson, eds. *The Definitive Visual Guide to the World's Wildlife.* New York: DK Publishing, 2001.

Mattison, C. *The Encyclopedia of Snakes.* New York: Facts on File, 1995.

Mehrtens, John M. *Living Snakes of the World in Color.* New York: Sterling Publishing, 1987.

Zug, G. R., L. J. Vitt, and J. P. Caldwell. *Herpetology: An Introductory Biology of Amphibians and Reptiles.* 2nd ed. San Diego: Academic Press, 2001.

Web sites

Cylindrophis maculates (Linne's Earth Snake) Linne 1754." Upeka Premaratne. http://members.fortunecity.com/ukp001/naja/cylindrophiidae/cylindrophis_maculatus.htm (accessed on September 22, 2004).

"Red-tailed Pipe Snake." Ecology Asia. http://www.ecologyasia.com/Vertebrates/red-tailed_pipe_snake.htm (accessed on September 22, 2004).

CHAPTER

phylum

class

subclass

order

monotypic order

suborder

▲ **family**

PHYSICAL CHARACTERISTICS

The false coral snake, the only species in this family, is a brightly colored, orange, red, or pinkish snake with fifty to sixty black bands. Each of the bands is two, three, or four scales wide. In some members of this species, the black bands are incomplete. In other words, they only reach partway up the sides of the snake and do not meet at the top of the back. Sometimes, the individual orange, red, or pinkish scales are outlined in black, making the snake look slightly speckled. Its belly is all red, orange, or pinkish, with no black banding. All scales on its body are shiny and smooth, which means they have no ridges, or keels. This nonvenomous (nahn-VEH-nuh-mus) snake looks somewhat similar to the venomous, or poisonous, coral snake species that shares its habitat and is therefore known as a "false" coral snake. Both false coral snakes and coral snakes, which are in the family Colubridae, are red, orange, or pink with evenly spaced black bands.

The body of a false coral snake is about the same thickness from one end to the other, giving the snake an overall tube shape. Both the head and tail are short. In snakes, the tail begins at the vent, which is a slitlike opening on the underside of the snake. This tube-shaped body is very similar to that of the pipe snakes of family Cylindrophiidae, and the false coral snakes are sometimes called red pipe snakes. At one time, in fact, the two families were combined into just one family. The only slight change in the body thickness of the false coral snake is in its head, which flattens out a bit. The head, which is made of very thick bones, has two small eyes covered by scales, and the large jaws have cone-shaped teeth that are very slightly curved. The snakes also have spurs, which are tiny, barely noticeable bits of bone that stick out near the vent. The snakes reach about 2 to 3 feet (0.6 to 1 meters) in length.

Within this species of false coral snake, scientists have named two subspecies, or races. A species has a two-part name, and the false coral snake is named *Anilius scytale*. When scientists name subspecies, they add a third name to the end of the scientific name. In the case of the false coral snakes, the two subspecies have slightly different scale patterns. *Anilius scytale scytale*, abbreviated to *A. s. scytale*, has more than 225 ventrals, which are the scales on its underside, and *A. s. phelpsorum* has fewer than 225. The belly scales in snakes are generally wider than the rest of the scales on the snake's sides and back. *A. s. scytale* also has black bands that are shorter than the red bands, while *A. s. phelpsorum* has black bands that are longer than the red bands. In addition, the two subspecies usually live in different areas, with *A. s. phelpsorum* living farther north than *A. s. scytale*. In some areas, such as northern Brazil and French Guiana, some individuals look a little bit like both subspecies, which means that their two parents may be from two different subspecies.

BONY MEMORIES

Some snakes, including false coral snakes, have spurs. These are tiny bits of bone that barely jut out near the vent, which is the slitlike opening on the underside of a snake. The spur is actually part of leftover hip and sometimes upper leg bones, carried down through the years from the long-ago ancestors of snakes, which had working hips and legs. The legs gradually disappeared, and in most snakes, the hips vanished, too. In the false coral snakes, however, the spurs are a reminder of past life on Earth.

GEOGRAPHIC RANGE

False coral snakes live in eastern Peru, Ecuador, Colombia, Bolivia, Brazil, French Guiana, southwestern Venezuela, Suriname, and Guyana, especially in the Amazon and Orinoco Basins, which are the areas surrounding the Amazon and Orinoco Rivers of South America.

HABITAT

This snake spends much of its time in burrows in loose soil. It lives in rainforests, especially in low-lying areas near streams or other waterways.

The false coral snake is a nonpoisonous snake and usually stays underground during the daytime. (Illustration by Jonathan Higgins. Reproduced by permission.)

DIET

False coral snakes eat long and narrow vertebrates (VER-teh-brehts), which are animals with backbones. These include small snakes, eels, caecilians, and amphisbaenians. Caecilians (seh-SEE-lee-ens) are salamanderlike animals that live underground. Amphisbaenians (am-fizz-BANE-ee-ens) are small-headed, short-tailed lizards that also make their homes below ground.

BEHAVIOR AND REPRODUCTION

This nonpoisonous snake is a burrower and usually stays underground during the daytime. When it is above ground and feels threatened, it will curl up its tail to show off its bright underside. The snake appears to be an ovoviviparous (oh-vo-vie-VIH-puh-rus) species, which means that the female produces eggs, but they hatch inside her, and she actually gives birth to baby snakes. Females have up to fifteen young at a time. Like many other snakes that stay buried under the ground much of the time, false coral snakes have been studied very little by scientists. Further information about their behavior and reproduction remains a mystery.

FALSE CORAL SNAKES AND PEOPLE

People and false coral snakes rarely see one another.

False coral snake (*Anilius scytale*)

CONSERVATION STATUS

The World Conservation Union (IUCN) considers the false coral snake to be Data Deficient, which means that scientists as yet have too little information to make a judgment about the threat of extinction. Destruction and other changes to their habitat, however, are probably threatening at least some populations.

FOR MORE INFORMATION

Books

Burnie, David, and Don Wilson, eds. *The Definitive Visual Guide to the World's Wildlife*. New York: DK Publishing, 2001.

Grace, Eric, ed. *Snakes*. San Francisco: Sierra Club Books for Children, 1994.

Greene, H. W. *Snakes: The Evolution of Mystery in Nature*. Berkeley: University of California Press, 1997.

Mehrtens, John M. *Living Snakes of the World in Color.* New York: Sterling Publishing, 1987.

Peters, J. A., R. Donoso-Barros, and P. E. Vanzolini. *Catalogue of the Neotropical Squamata.* Part 1, *Snakes.* Washington, DC: Smithsonian Institution Press, 1986.

Zug, G. R., L. J. Vitt, and J. P. Caldwell. *Herpetology: An Introductory Biology of Amphibians and Reptiles,* 2nd ed. San Diego: Academic Press, 2001.

Web sites

"Family Aniliidae." EMBL (European Molecular Biology Laboratory) Reptile Database. http://www.embl-heidelberg.de/uetz/families/Aniliidae .html (accessed on September 28, 2004).

Lovera, A. "*Anilius scytale* (false coral snake, pipe snake, and red pipe snake)." Animal Diversity Web. http://animaldiversity.ummz.umich.edu/ site/accounts/information/Anilius_scytale.html (accessed on February 2, 2005).

"Pipe Snake (*Anilius scytale*). Animal Planet.com. http://animal.discovery .com/fansites/jeffcorwin/carnival/slithering/pipesnake.html (accessed on February 2, 2005).

Class: Reptilia

Order: Squamata

Suborder: Serpentes

Family: Xenopeltidae

Number of species: 2 species

family
CHAPTER

PHYSICAL CHARACTERISTICS

The two species of sunbeam snakes—the common sunbeam snake and the Hainan sunbeam snake—are among the world's most beautiful snakes. Their metallic-looking bodies shine different colors depending on how light bounces off them. When a sunbeam snake is in the shade, its back looks dark purplish brown or black, but when it slithers out into the sun, the large scales on its back and head erupt into a wave of color. Like a raindrop can bend sunlight to create a rainbow, this snake has scales that reflect sunlight into many colors. This property is called iridescence (IH-rih-DEH-sense). In fact, another common name for this snake is the iridescent earth snake. Young snakes, which are also iridescent, often have a white patch, or collar, on the upper neck.

Adults have slightly flattened bodies that are white, light gray, or light yellow on the bottom. The light color also extends up onto the lip scales. Sunbeam snakes have very small eyes on a head that is about the same diameter as the neck, so the head is not as obvious as it is in vipers, pythons, and many other snakes. The head flattens out toward the snout, giving it a wedge shape suited for digging. The skeleton also has some interesting features. The bone in the front of the upper jaw has teeth where most snakes do not. The snake's teeth are also all hinged at the base, rather than more firmly attached to the jaw bone, so they can wiggle back and forth a bit without falling out.

Adults usually reach about 2 to 3 feet (0.6 to 0.9 meters) in length. The tail makes up about one-tenth of the body's total

phylum

class

subclass

order

monotypic order

suborder

▲ **family**

"OLD" SPECIES

Scientists sometimes refer to some species, such as the sunbeam snakes, as being relicts (REH-lihkts). Relict species are those that now live in a much smaller area than they once did. Typically, they have been on Earth for a very long time compared to other similar animals and have a set of features—usually something in the skeleton—that is similar to that seen in ancient animals, many of which are known only from their fossils. In some cases, relicts now live in widely separated areas, because the species in between died out over the years.

length. In snakes, the tail begins at the vent, a slitlike opening on the belly side.

GEOGRAPHIC RANGE

Sunbeam snakes live in southern China and Southeast Asia from the Nicobar and Andaman islands west of Thailand to the Philippines and south through much of Indonesia.

HABITAT

Sunbeam snakes spend at least part of their time underground, hidden in leaves or under trash. They live in humid forests, as well as rice paddies, farm fields, parks, and gardens next to the woods. People rarely see them deep in the forests, which may mean they do not travel there, but it may also simply mean people usually overlook them in that habitat.

DIET

Scientists have only studied the diet of the common sunbeam snake, which eats lizards, frogs, and snakes, as well as small mammals and birds. The snake is a very fast eater, swallowing its prey more quickly than most other snakes can. Scientists have not studied the other species.

BEHAVIOR AND REPRODUCTION

These snakes are nonvenomous (nahn-VEH-nuh-mus), or not poisonous. They stay out of sight most of the day, remaining underground in burrows. A sunbeam snake uses its wedge-shaped head to push through leaves, litter, and loose soil. Although it is capable of digging, it usually uses burrows made by other animals rather than making them itself. The snakes become more active at night and leave the burrows to hunt. They seem to keep up their guards when out at night, moving quickly with the head pressed against the ground and the tongue flicking about again and again to pick up any scents of other animals in the air. When they feel threatened, sunbeam snakes will shake the tail like a rattlesnake does, but the sunbeam snakes have no rattles, so the tail makes no noise. Nonetheless, scientists believe that the motion alone is enough to make an attacker, also known as a predator (PREH-duh-ter), think twice about approaching the snake. Predators that come too close are greeted by a very bad-smelling material that oozes from the snake's vent area. If the predator actually touches the sunbeam snake, the snake will stiffen its body and jerk about wildly. Again, while this poses no danger to the attacker, the motion may be enough to cause the predator to leave the snake alone.

Female sunbeam snakes lay up to seventeen eggs at a time. Scientists know little else about their reproduction.

SUNBEAM SNAKES AND PEOPLE

Sunbeam snakes and people leave one another alone for the most part, but the snakes are starting to become more popular in the pet trade as more people become familiar with their color-changing scales. They make poor pets, however, because they remain underground most of the time and usually give off a bad odor when handled. They also are very nervous, and the stress is likely one reason they often die soon after they are purchased. In addition, the snakes do not reproduce well in captivity, which means that people must hunt them in the wild to supply the pet trade, rather than raise babies from already captured snakes.

CONSERVATION STATUS

These snakes are not listed as endangered or threatened.

Common sunbeam snake *(Xenopeltis unicolor)*

COMMON SUNBEAM SNAKE
Xenopeltis unicolor

Physical characteristics: The common sunbeam snake has a dark purplish brown back, but its smooth scales shine in blues, greens, reds, and yellows when the animal slithers out on a bright, sunny day. Its belly is whitish. That whitish color extends into a collar around the back of the head and front of the neck in juveniles. The snakes have wedged-shaped heads that help them to dig into the soil. Adults usually reach less than 3 feet (0.9 meters) in length, but some can grow to 49 inches (1.25 meters).

Geographic range: The common sunbeam snake lives in southern China and Southeast Asia.

Habitat: The common sunbeam snake is semifossorial (SEM-ee-faw-SOR-ee-ul). "Fossorial" means it lives below ground, and the term "semi" means they only spend part of their time there. They are most often seen at the edges of forests or in the farm fields and neighborhoods nearby.

Diet: In the wild, they eat lizards, especially skinks, as well as frogs, snakes, small mammals, and small birds. Captive snakes will eat mice.

Behavior and reproduction: This snake stays underground much of the day and comes out at night to hunt. In captivity, it kills mice by constriction (kun-STRIK-shun), which is the ability to squeeze a prey animal until it cannot breathe and therefore dies. When threatened, the common sunbeam snake will shake its tail and, if touched, will jerk its body. Females lay up to seventeen eggs at a time, and eggs reportedly hatch in about seven to eight weeks, but scientists know little else about its reproduction.

Sunbeam snakes spend at least part of their time underground, hidden in leaves or under trash. (Illustration by Jonathan Higgins. Reproduced by permission.)

Common sunbeam snakes and people: The common sunbeam snake and people leave one another alone.

Conservation status: This snake is not listed as endangered or threatened. ■

FOR MORE INFORMATION

Books

Burnie, David, and Don Wilson, eds. *The Definitive Visual Guide to the World's Wildlife.* New York: DK Publishing, 2001.

Campden-Main, S. M. *A Field Guide to the Snakes of South Vietnam.* Washington, DC: Smithsonian Institution, 1970.

Cox, M. J. *The Snakes of Thailand and Their Husbandry.* Malabar, FL: Krieger Publishing Company, 1991.

Deuve, J. *Serpents du Laos.* Paris: ORSTOM, 1970.

Grace, Eric, ed. *Snakes.* San Francisco: Sierra Club Books for Children, 1994.

Mehrtens, John M. *Living Snakes of the World in Color.* New York: Sterling Publishing, 1987.

Taylor, Barbara. *Snakes.* New York: Lorenz, 1998.

Zug, G. R., L. J. Vitt, and J. P. Caldwell. *Herpetology: An Introductory Biology of Amphibians and Reptiles,* 2nd ed. San Diego: Academic Press, 2001.

Web sites

"Sunbeam Snake (Iridescent Earth Snake)." Ecology Asia. http://www
.ecologyasia.com/Vertebrates/sunbeam_snake.htm (accessed on
September 21, 2004).

"Sunbeam Snake (*Xenopeltis unicolor*)." Science Museums of China.
http://smc.kisti.re.kr/animal/class/cls310.html (accessed on September
21, 2004).

"Sunbeam Snake or Iridescent Earth Snake." Wild Singapore. http://www
.wildsingapore.per.sg/discovery/factsheet/snakesunbeam.htm (accessed
on September 21, 2004).

**NEOTROPICAL SUNBEAM
SNAKE**

Loxocemidae

Class: Reptilia

Order: Testudines

Family: Loxocemidae

One species: Neotropical sunbeam
snake (*Loxocemus
bicolor*)

PHYSICAL CHARACTERISTICS

This family has only one species, the neotropical sunbeam snake. It also is known as a Mexican burrowing python, New World python, ground python, dwarf python, and burrowing boa, but it is actually neither a boa nor a python. Boas and pythons are in separate families. For many years, some researchers felt this snake was similar enough to the boas that it should be placed in the Boidae family, but now most agree that it should have its own family, as it does in this chapter.

The neotropical sunbeam snake has a small mouth, tiny cat-eyed pupils, and a somewhat-pointed, upturned snout. Its head is covered with larger scales than the rest of the upper body. The belly side of the snake is whitish, while the upper snake is brown, sometimes with small, white speckles. This obvious shift from the brown back to the white underside gives the snake its scientific name *bicolor* ("bi" meaning two). Its scales are slightly iridescent (IH-rih-DEH-sent), which means that they change color depending on how light bounces off them. Often, the neotropical sunbeam snake is confused with another family of snakes that lives in southeast Asia. The southeast Asian sunbeam snakes have iridescent scales much like those on the neotropical sunbeam snakes. One feature that helps to tell them apart is the presence of pelvic spurs, which are tiny bits of bone that stick out from the underside of neotropical sunbeam snakes near the vent, which is the slitlike opening on the belly side between the middle and end of the snake. Asian sunbeam snakes do not have spurs. Male neotropical sunbeam snakes have two

phylum

class

subclass

order

monotypic order

suborder

▲ **family**

noticeable pelvic spurs. Females also have spurs, but they are small and difficult to see. Young snakes look like smaller versions of the adults. They have the slightly iridescent, copper-colored skin, but they do not have any white speckles on their backs.

Neotropical sunbeam snakes have heavy muscular bodies. Adults usually are less than 3 feet (1 meter) long, but large ones can reach 5 feet (1.5 meters) in length. The short tail makes up only about 10 to 14 percent of its total body length. As in all snakes, the tail begins at the vent.

GEOGRAPHIC RANGE

This snake lives from southwestern Mexico through much of Central America, including Guatemala, El Salvador, Honduras, Nicaragua, and northwestern Costa Rica.

HABITAT

Neotropical sunbeam snakes live in warm climates and a variety of forested areas, but not in the mountains. They also sometimes make their home along the beaches of the coastline. They are secretive animals that hide among rocks and leaves, beneath logs and/or under their bark, in below-ground holes, and even in ant nests.

DIET

This snake will eat small mammals and adult and young lizards, including whip-tailed lizards. It also eats the eggs of black and green iguanas and olive Ridley seaturtles. The snake apparently crawls into the lizard and turtle nests, wraps its body around the eggs, then moves in with its head to swallow them whole. In captivity, the snakes will sometimes bite into the eggs, but then swallow the entire egg. A snake may eat several eggs, sometimes more than two dozen, at one time.

BEHAVIOR AND REPRODUCTION

Because this snake spends a good deal of its time underground, scientists know little about the details of its behavior in the wild

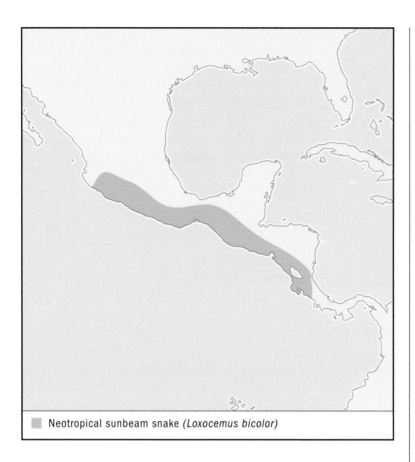

Neotropical sunbeam snake (*Loxocemus bicolor*)

but have learned some information from captive snakes, which are held in various zoos around the world. They are called semi-fossorial (SEM-ee-faw-SOR-ee-ul) animals. "Fossorial" means that they spend time below ground, and adding "semi" points out that they frequently leave their underground homes. During the daytime, the snakes stay out of sight by using their upward-curved snouts to push through leaves to reach the ground, where they dig into loose dirt to make tunnels, or burrows. They come out at night and on rainy days to wander around above ground looking for things to eat. The white speckles on the backs of adults likely provide some camouflage. Like many other animals, the pattern on the skin breaks up the outline of their bodies and makes it more difficult for predators (PREH-duh-ters), or animals that hunt other animals for food, to spot them against the background habitat. For example, a completely dark snake slithering over a pile of leaves would be more noticeable than a snake with lighter patches that hide its outline.

The neotropical sunbeam snake finds its food by following scent trails or by simply spotting a mammal, lizard, or an egg. It is a constrictor (kun-STRIK-tuhr), which means that it coils its body around the animal it wants to eat, then tightens the coil until the animal passes out or dies. It then releases the coil, slides its head around, and eats the prey. As noted, it wraps its body around eggs but does not crush them.

During breeding season, male neotropical sunbeam snakes fight over females, sometimes biting one another in quite vicious battles. The males have sharp spurs near the vent. These spurs can apparently cut the female quite deeply during mating. About two months after mating, captive females commonly lay from two to four eggs at a time, although they can lay eight or more. Baby snakes in the wild hatch in May. When they reach four to five years old, they can begin to have their own babies.

NEOTROPICAL SUNBEAM SNAKES AND PEOPLE

This is not a typical pet species, probably because of its tendency to spend much of its time underground. The Convention on International Trade in Endangered Species (CITES) lists this species as one that people cannot freely buy and sell.

CONSERVATION STATUS

This species is not listed as endangered or threatened.

FOR MORE INFORMATION

Books

Burnie, David, and Don Wilson, eds. *The Definitive Visual Guide to the World's Wildlife.* New York: DK Publishing, 2001.

Greene, H. W. *Snakes: The Evolution of Mystery in Nature.* Berkeley: University of California Press, 1997.

McDiarmid, R. W., J. A. Campbell, and T. Touré. *Snake Species of the World.* Vol. 1. *A Taxonomic and Geographic Reference.* Washington, DC: The Herpetologists' League, 1999.

Savage, J. M. *The Amphibians and Reptiles of Costa Rica.* Chicago: University of Chicago Press, 2002.

Wilson, L. D., and J. R. Meyer. *The Snakes of Honduras.* 2nd ed. Milwaukee: Milwaukee Public Museum, 1985.

Web sites

"New World Sunbeam Snake." Vida Preciosa International Inc. http://www.vpi.com/5VPIBreeders/NewWorldSunbeamSnake/ NewWorldSunbeamSnake.htm (accessed on September 11, 2004).

"Mexican Burrowing Python, *Loxocemus*." Glasgow Zoopark. http://www .glasgowzoo.co.uk/articles/coldblooded/mexburrowingpyth.php (accessed on September 11, 2004).

"Mexican Burrowing Snake." Utah's Hogle Zoo. http://www.hoglezoo .org/animals/view.php?id=42 (accessed on September 11, 2004).

Other sources

"Convention on International Trade in Endangered Species of Wild Fauna and Flora." http://www.cites.org (accessed on September 9, 2004).

BOAS

Boidae

Class: Reptilia

Order: Squamata

Family: Boidae

Number of species: 41 species

family

CHAPTER

phylum

class

subclass

order

monotypic order

suborder

▲ **family**

PHYSICAL CHARACTERISTICS

Boas come in many sizes, from small to very large. The adults of some species grow to less than 1 foot (about 0.3 meters) in length, but some are immense. The boa constrictor (kun-STRIK-tuhr), for example, reaches nearly 14 feet (4.3 meters) in length, and the green anaconda can grow to 25 feet (7.7 meters) in length and 300 pounds (136 kilograms). Among all the boa species, females are usually larger than males.

The boas are split into two subfamilies. One includes the sand boa, rubber boa, rosy boa, and eleven other species, none of which grows to much more than 4 feet (1.2 meters) in length. They all have small eyes, narrow heads on thick necks, large scales on the end of their snouts, and short tails. The tail in a snake is the part of the body behind the vent, a crosswise opening on the belly side of the snake and toward the rear of the animal. The other subfamily includes the anacondas, boa constrictors, and other mostly larger snakes. The smallest is the Abaco boa, which reaches just 31.5 inches (81 centimeters) in length, and the largest is the green anaconda, which can be about ten times as long. Members of this subfamily have large heads on smaller necks, large eyes, and long tails. The anacondas are different in that they have distinctively soft and loose skin.

Depending on the species, boas may be red, orange, yellow, green, brown, or gray and may or may not have patterns of blotches or spots on their backs. Some have scales that shine in different colors when the light strikes them in certain ways, and, in a few, the color of the skin changes completely from dark in the daytime to light at night. For example, the Fiji Island boa can switch from black to pale pink within six hours. Two features that all boas share are the presence of heat sensors on the front of the face and two little bits of bone, known as spurs, that look like small claws. One spur lies on each side of the vent. The spurs are always noticeable in males but are sometimes small and not easily seen in females.

GEOGRAPHIC RANGE

Boas live in many places around the world, including South America, Central America, North America, Europe, Africa, and Asia. They are also present in New Guinea and on many islands throughout their range.

HABITAT

From fields to forests and marshes to deserts, boas live in many different habitats. Some of the sand boas make their homes in deserts, while others, like the viper boas, live in wet forests. Some species prefer warm climates, but others are able to exist in very cold areas, like southern Mongolia in Asia. The boa constrictor is unusual in that it can survive well in a wide variety of habitats, from deserts to rainforests in warmer climates and also grasslands in cooler areas.

DIET

While boas may spend some time slinking through their habitats looking for animals to eat, most of them are ambush hunters, which means that they find a good spot, wait motionless for a prey animal to wander by, and then strike out to grab it. The heat sensors on their faces help them "see" the heat coming from the prey, which helps them to hunt at night. The sand boas ambush prey by burying themselves in the sand and waiting for lizards or small mammals. Amazon tree boas coil around tree branches to ambush birds, and Puerto Rican boas sit still in the entrances to caves and watch for bats. Green anacondas, which are also called water boas, often lurk underwater until a passing fish or other animal comes within striking distance. Members of the boa family are constrictors, which means that the snake will kill its prey by looping its body around the animal and squeezing, cutting off the animal's air until it is dead. While most boas eat small mammals, birds, or reptiles, the green anaconda and a few of the giant species eat quite large animals, including deer and crocodilelike caimans

A BIG MOUTHFUL

People are often surprised that a snake that looks so small can even get its mouth around what look to be impossibly large animals that make up its diet. A green anaconda, for example, can eat an entire deer. Snakes are able to do it, in part, because their lower jaws are different from those in a human. Unlike a person's lower jaw, a snake's jaw is split into left and right sides that are connected by stretchy muscle and tissue, called ligament (LIH-guh-ment). As the snake's teeth grasp the prey animal and draw it into the mouth, the lower jaw—one side at a time—moves forward and pulls the animal farther inside. The snake's head and then its neck stretch like elastic to become much wider than normal, so the prey can fit inside its body.

(KAY-muhns). Some reports, although extremely rare, indicate that green anacondas have killed and eaten humans.

BEHAVIOR AND REPRODUCTION

Boas frequently come out during the day to sunbathe, or bask, which warms their bodies. They are most active, however, at night. Some of their most interesting behaviors are seen in the ways they defend themselves. When threatened, many sand boa species roll the body into a ball with the head buried in the middle, and some of the short-tailed species poke out the tail to trick the attacker into thinking it is actually the head. The snake can survive a bite to the tail much better than a bite to the head. The Fiji Island boa flattens its head and neck much like a cobra, which makes the snake look bigger and may frighten off an attacker. Some of the larger boas hiss, strike, and bite when they feel threatened. They may also ooze a bad-smelling material from the vent area.

During breeding season, the males of some species wrestle over females, sometimes biting one another. In most species, the females give birth to baby snakes. A few, like the Calabar ground boa (sometimes mistakenly called a ground python, which confuses it with the python family), lay eggs.

BOAS AND PEOPLE

Many of the smaller species have little contact with humans. Some people hunt the larger boas for their skins and/or meat or to make medicines. Several species are popular in the pet trade.

CONSERVATION STATUS

According to the World Conservation Union (IUCN), one species is Endangered, facing a very high risk of extinction in the wild in the near future. In addition, four are Vulnerable, which means that they face a high risk of extinction in the wild in the near future, and two are Near Threatened and are at risk of becoming threatened with extinction in the wild in the future.

The U.S. Fish and Wildlife Service lists three species as Endangered. The low numbers of these snakes result from loss of their habitat and, in the case of the endangered Mona boa, from cats and rats that have been introduced to the area and prey on the snakes. In addition to these listed snakes, one species may be extinct, that is, no longer alive. Scientists have only one record of this species, called Cropan's boa or *Corallus cropanii*, which dates back to the mid-1900s.

Boa constrictor (*Boa constrictor*)

BOA CONSTRICTOR
Boa constrictor

Physical characteristics: Boa constrictors are usually brown with darker brown and somewhat triangular markings running down the back. The markings may become reddish on the tail, which explains their other common name: redtail boa. The snakes have heads that are wider than their necks and long tails that they use to cling to tree branches. Boas can become quite large, with the longest reaching 13.8 feet (4.2 meters).

Geographic range: They are found in Mexico, throughout Central America, in much of South America, and on various nearby islands along the coasts of these areas.

Habitat: The boa constrictor lives in many habitats, including evergreen and deciduous jungles, rainforests, near-desert areas, grasslands, and farm fields. Boas are good climbers and are often found in trees.

Diet: Boa constrictors usually dine on small mammals, like rats and squirrels, but also on birds, iguanas (ee-GWA-nuhs), and other large lizards. Large boas, which do most of their hunting on the ground, sometimes eat bigger animals, such as porcupines. Young boas are much more likely than adults to hunt for prey in trees.

Behavior and reproduction: Boas hunt for food mostly at night, spending the day inside cracks in tree trunks, in burrows made by tunneling animals, or in some other hiding place. Scientists know little about their mating behavior in the wild. Females, which give birth to baby snakes rather than eggs, may have twenty-one to sixty-one young at a time. The babies are about 19.5 inches (49.5 centimeters) long at birth. The young can have their own young once they are two to four years old.

Boa constrictors and people: Boa constrictors are rather common in the pet trade. They are often seen in farm fields, where the snakes find, kill, and eat many pest animals.

Conservation status: This snake is not endangered or threatened. ■

Emerald tree boa *(Corallus caninus)*

EMERALD TREE BOA
Corallus caninus

Physical characteristics: The emerald tree boa has a bright green back with white, diamond-shaped markings. The snakes have large, almost heart-shaped heads and long tails. They are not venomous (VEH-nuh-mus), that is, not poisonous, but have long front teeth—sometimes up to 1.5 inches (3.8 centimeters). Adults can grow to about 7.3 feet (2.2 meters) in length.

Geographic range: The emerald tree boa lives in the northern half of South America, near the Amazon River.

Habitat: This tropical species spends most of its life in trees, often in those with branches that hang over rivers.

Diet: An ambush hunter, the emerald tree boa waits patiently in trees for birds or small mammals, including monkeys, to approach. It then strikes out, grasps the animal with its long front teeth, and wraps its prey with its strong body. It then squeezes the animal to death before eating it.

Behavior and reproduction: This snake spends most of its time coiled around or looped over branches in trees. From this perch, it watches for a passing bird or other animal for its next meal. This is a live-bearing species, which means that the females give birth to baby snakes rather than laying eggs. The babies are often red or orange, but sometimes green. All change to green as they get older.

Emerald tree boas and people: Emerald tree boas are sought in the pet trade, but laws are helping to protect them in many countries.

Conservation status: This species is not endangered or threatened.

■

The emerald tree boa waits patiently in trees for birds or small mammals to approach. It then strikes out, grasps the animal with its long front teeth, and wraps its prey with its strong body. It then squeezes the animal to death before eating it. (Illustration by Marguette Dongvillo. Reproduced by permission.)

Green anaconda (Eunectes murinus)

GREEN ANACONDA
Eunectes murinus

Physical characteristics: A long and large-bodied snake, the green anaconda can reach a length of 25 feet (7.6 meters) and 300 pounds (136 kilograms). An average adult is about 10 to 15 feet (3 to 4.6 meters). It is a dark green snake with round, black spots down the back and a black stripe behind each eye.

Geographic range: This snake lives in the northern half of South America and on the West Indies island of Trinidad.

Habitat: Also known as the water boa, the green anaconda is often found in freshwater marshes, swamps, ponds, and slow-moving

The green anaconda can reach lengths of 25 feet (7.6 meters) and 300 pounds (136 kilograms). (Joe McDonald/Bruce Coleman Inc. Reproduced by permission.)

streams or along their shores. The young often climb onto low branches along the water's edge.

Diet: Prey include birds, fish, turtles, crocodilelike caimans, and mammals, such as deer and monkeys. The snake kills the animals by coiling its body around them and squeezing.

Behavior and reproduction: Green anacondas are ambush hunters, waiting in the water near the shoreline for prey animals to approach. They sometimes wander onto land to sunbathe, or bask. The breeding season is in the dry season, when several males will approach a female for a chance to mate with her. The females give birth to twenty to forty-five baby snakes. Some of the young can be quite large, ranging from about 2 to 3 feet (61 to 91.4 centimeters) in length.

Green anacondas and people: Green anacondas and people have little contact. Their large size and bad temper make them poor pets. Although green anacondas can and do eat humans on extremely rare occasions, most stories of such activity are untrue.

Conservation status: This species is not endangered or threatened. ■

FOR MORE INFORMATION

Books:

Brazaitis, P., and M. Watanabe. *Snakes of the World.* New York: Crescent Books, 1992.

Cleave, Andrew. *Snakes and Reptiles: A Portrait of the Animal World.* New York: Magna Books, 1994.

de Vosjoli, Philippe, Roger Klingenberg, and Jeff Ronne. *The Boa Constrictor Manual.* Santee, CA: Advanced Vivarium Systems, 1998.

Greene, Harry W. *Snakes: The Evolution of Mystery in Nature.* Berkeley: University of California Press, 1997.

Lamar, W. *The World's Most Spectacular Reptiles and Amphibians.* Tampa, FL: World Publications, 1997.

Martin, James. *Boa Constrictors.* Minneapolis, MN: Capstone Press, 1996.

Minton, Sherman A., and Madge Rutherford Minton. *Giant Reptiles.* New York: Scribners, 1973.

Murphy, John C., and Robert W. Henderson. *Tales of Giant Snakes: A Historical Natural History of Anacondas and Pythons.* Malabar, FL: Krieger Publishing, 1997.

O'Shea, Mark. *A Guide to the Snakes of Papua New Guinea.* Port Moresby, Papua New Guinea: Independent Publishing, 1996.

Pope, Clifford Millhouse. *The Giant Snakes: The Natural History of the Boa Constrictor, the Anaconda, and the Largest Pythons, Including Comparative Facts about Other Snakes and Basic Information on Reptiles in General.* New York: Knopf, 1961.

Stafford, Peter J., and Robert W. Henderson. *Kaleidoscopic Tree Boas: The Genus Corallus of Tropical America.* Malabar, FL: Krieger, 1996.

Stebbins, Robert C. *A Field Guide to the Western Reptiles and Amphibians: Field Marks of All Species in Western North America, Including Baja California.* 2nd ed. Boston: Houghton Mifflin, 1985.

Tolson, P. J., and R. W. Henderson. *The Natural History of West Indian Boas.* Taunton, U.K.: R & A Publishing, 1993.

Web sites:

"Anaconda." Nashville Zoo. http://www.nashvillezoo.org/ anaconda.htm (accessed on September 17, 2004).

"Boa constrictor." Enchanted Learning.com. http://www.enchantedlearning .com/subjects/reptiles/snakes/Boa.shtml (accessed on September 17, 2004).

"In the Dark." Animal Planet.com. http://animal.discovery.com/ convergence/snakes/dispatches/dispatch2.html (accessed on September 17, 2004).

PYTHONS

Pythonidae

Class: Reptilia

Order: Squamata

Suborder: Serpentes

Family: Pythonidae

Number of species: 32 species

family

CHAPTER

PHYSICAL CHARACTERISTICS

Some of the largest snakes in the world are pythons. One, the reticulated python, even holds the world's record for the longest wild snake at 33 feet (10.1 meters). That particular snake was killed in 1912 in Sulawesi, also known as Celebes, in Indonesia. Besides the reticulated python, however, only two other pythons grow to be longer than 20 feet (6.1 meters). In fact, the pygmy pythons of Australia are less than 2 feet (61 centimeters) long when full grown.

Pythons look much like boas. They both have cat's-eye pupils and little claw-like bits of bone, known as spurs, on each side of the vent, which is the slitlike opening on the belly side of the snake. They both also have heat vision and can "see" heat with little pits on the scales of their lips. Pythons and boas differ, however, in the location of these pits. In boas, they fall between scales, but a python's pits are in the middle of the scales. Both use the heat sensors to help them locate prey or food animals. Another major difference between the pythons and boas is that all pythons lay eggs, while all but three species of boas give birth to baby snakes.

Some pythons are almost completely one color, but many have patterns of blotches or bands on their backs. Often, the snake's scales are iridescent (IH-rih-DEH-sent), which means that they shine different colors depending on how the light hits them. A number of these snakes, including the Papuan python, can actually change color. This species can switch from having a bright yellow body and light gray head to completely dark brown from head to tail.

phylum

class

subclass

order

monotypic order

suborder

▲ **family**

SEVEN NEW PYTHON SPECIES

In 2000 and 2001, the number of python species grew by seven. The seven new species resulted not when someone found a new snake in the field, but when scientists decided that they had wrongly lumped those seven species in with other python species. Once they were removed and given new species names, the python family grew from twenty-five species to thirty-two. As studies into this family continue, scientists expect that they may find more species hidden inside the thirty-two, and the python family will grow yet again.

GEOGRAPHIC RANGE

Pythons are found in southern Asia; southeastern China and Southeast Asia; the Philippines; Papua, New Guinea, and Indonesia; and Australia. They also live in the central and southern region of Africa, which is known as Sub-Saharan Africa.

HABITAT

Depending on the species, pythons may live in thick forests, open forests, rainforests, rocky and scrubby areas high on hillsides, deserts, grasslands, swamps, or other freshwater areas. Some stay on land all their lives, while others spend much of their time climbing in trees. A few survive quite well in the desert, but others prefer the wetter areas, living in rainforests, or in some cases actually in a lake or other water area for up to six months a year.

DIET

Pythons are meat eaters and mostly feed on mammals and lizards, although some may take an occasional bird, and a few enjoy other species of snakes. They may crawl around looking for prey animals, but more often than not, they hunt by ambush. To ambush a prey, the snake remains still and waits for an animal to happen by and then lashes out to grab it.

Although it is very, very rare, some of the largest python species, including reticulated, African, and Indian pythons, have been known to coil around and then eat humans.

BEHAVIOR AND REPRODUCTION

Constriction (kun-STRIK-shun) is one of this family's best-known behaviors. After grabbing a prey animal in its jaws, the python wraps its body around the animal and constricts or squeezes so hard that the prey cannot breathe. When the animal dies or passes out, the snake uncoils and moves its head around to swallow the meal whole.

When they feel threatened, many will hiss, ooze a bad-smelling material from the vent area at the beginning of the tail, and possibly strike and/or bite. The ball python gets its name because it curls up in a ball when it feels it is in danger.

Pythons are mostly active at night, although they often will sunbathe, or bask, during the daytime in a warm spot. One species, the diamond python of Australia, hibernates, or enters a deep sleep, during the winter to survive the cold months. Scientists know little more about python behavior.

Pythons are an egg laying species. Females of small species, such as the pygmy python, lay up to ten eggs at a time. Larger females, such as the reticulated python, may lay more than one hundred. The eggs usually stick together in a clump. Females coil their bodies around the eggs, which protects them from other animals and keeps them warm. Some mothers can even heat up their bodies during this time by tightening and loosening the muscles. Occasionally, a female may leave the eggs while she goes out to sunbathe and then return to wrap the eggs in her heated body. Once the eggs hatch, the baby snakes usually look much like the adults, although they are sometimes more brightly colored.

PYTHONS AND PEOPLE

People hunt pythons for their meat and skin and to make folk medicines. They are also popular in the pet trade, but most of the pet snakes now are born from other captive snakes rather than taken from the wild. Although some of the largest species are able to kill and eat humans, this hardly ever happens.

CONSERVATION STATUS

According to the World Conservation Union (IUCN), Ramsey's python of Australia is Endangered, which means that it faces a very high risk of extinction in the wild. The Asiatic rock python is listed as Near Threatened, which means that it is likely to qualify for a threatened category in the near future. The U.S. Fish and Wildlife Service also lists a certain group, called a subspecies, of the Indian python as Endangered, or in danger of extinction throughout all or a significant portion of its range. Overcollecting is a major problem for these snakes, and many countries now have strict rules in place to protect the pythons.

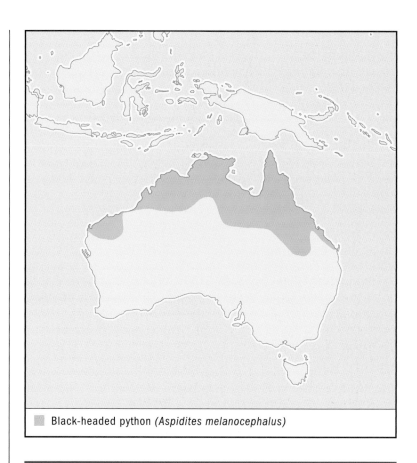

Black-headed python (*Aspidites melanocephalus*)

BLACK-HEADED PYTHON
Aspidites melanocephalus

Physical characteristics: The black-headed python has a shiny black head and neck on a beige body. Its body is striped with medium-to-dark brown bands. Adults usually reach no more than 5 feet (1.5 meters) in length.

Geographic range: This species lives across northern Australia.

Habitat: This snake usually remains in wooded areas, but some travel into rainforests, grasslands, and dry and rocky areas.

Diet: Black-headed pythons eat mostly lizards and other snakes, including venomous (VEH-nuh-mus) or poisonous species. They will also eat birds and mammals once in a while.

Black-headed pythons eat mostly lizards and other snakes, including venomous species. (Illustration by Brian Cressman. Reproduced by permission.)

Behavior and reproduction: Active at night, this species spends part of its time in tunnels, or burrows, made by other animals. It is also able to dig burrows itself. The females, which are usually larger than the males, lay up to eighteen eggs at a time. Each egg measures about 3.5 inches (8.9 centimeters) long and hatches into a baby snake of approximately 2 feet (61 centimeters) in length. The babies look much like the adults but are more brightly colored. After four or five years, the young are old enough to have their own babies.

Black-headed pythons and people: Because it lives far away from people, the black-headed python and people rarely see or bother one another.

Conservation status: Although the World Conservation Union (IUCN) does not list it as threatened, scientists know little about the number of these snakes or how well they are surviving. ■

Green python (Morelia viridis)

GREEN PYTHON
Morelia viridis

Physical characteristics: The green python is bright green in color and may have a pattern of small blue markings, sometimes forming a thin stripe down its back. It may also have a few white, yellow, and/or black scales scattered here and there on the green back. It has long straight front teeth and a long tail. Adults usually range from 4.5 to 6 feet (1.4 to 1.8 meters) in length; a few reach more than 7 feet (2.1 meters).

Geographic range: The green python lives in New Guinea and several nearby islands. A small group also makes its home on the Cape York Peninsula of far northeastern Australia.

Habitat: The green python, which is also known as the green tree python, lives in forests, often climbing up and through tree branches.

Diet: Although they are capable of climbing, adults usually hunt on the ground. They eat mainly rats and other rodents, although they will also feed on a bird occasionally, capturing it with their long teeth. Young snakes, in particular, eat lizards.

Behavior and reproduction: This snake rests in branches much of the time by looping its body back and forth over a branch and drooping its head downward. This pose almost looks as if someone had rolled the snake into a spiral and carefully laid it over the limb. The snake is most active at night and does the majority of its hunting then. In one of its hunting tactics, it keeps its body still while wiggling just the tip of its tail. The motion lures in lizards, which the snake attacks and kills. Females, which are usually larger than males, have up to thirty eggs at a time. The 1.6–inch (4–centimeter) eggs hatch into young snakes that are 11 to 14 inches (28 to 36 centimeters) long. Young snakes may be bright red with scattered yellow and white scales or vivid yellow with small red and white markings. They switch to green as they grow older. Once they reach three years old, the young can start having their own babies.

Green pythons and people: Some people hunt this snake for its meat.

Conservation status: This snake is not considered endangered or threatened. ■

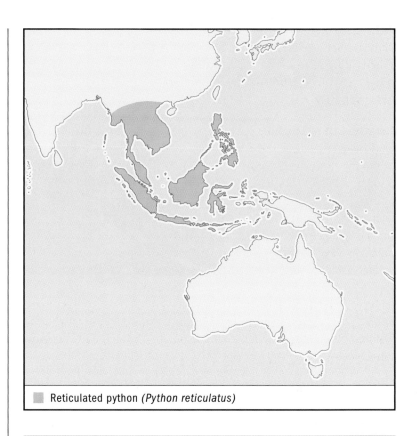

Reticulated python *(Python reticulatus)*

RETICULATED PYTHON
Python reticulatus

Physical characteristics: One of the largest snake species known, the reticulated python can reach as much as 33 feet (10.1 meters) long. Normally, however, adults are about 12 to 15 feet (3.7 to 4.6 meters), although 20-foot (6.1-meter) individuals are often found. The snake has a beautifully patterned back of yellow, black, and brown.

Geographic range: Its range includes the Philippines and Indonesia, India's Nicobar Islands, and much of Southeast Asia.

Habitat: The reticulated python usually lives in or near freshwater swamps, rivers, and lakes, often making its home in thick or open forests, caves, or rocky areas.

Diet: Also known as the regal python, it eats many animals, including monkeys, rats and other rodents, dogs and cats, pigs, deer, lizards, and large birds. They will also kill and eat humans, although this is very rare.

Behavior and reproduction: This snake spends a good deal of its time either climbing in trees or swimming in the water. It tends to be more active at night, especially if it lives near people. It rests in hiding places, such as burrows made by other animals, or inside hollow logs. The reticulated python hunts by either sneaking up on an animal or by remaining still and letting the animal come to it. Large females can lay more than one hundred eggs at a time, while smaller females lay less than two dozen. Each egg, which measures 4 to 5 inches (10 to 13 centimeters) long, hatches into a 2- to 3-foot (61- to 91-centimeter) baby snake. The babies look like the adults. Once the young snakes reach their third or fourth year, they are old enough to start having babies of their own.

One of the largest snake species known, the reticulated python can reach as much as 33 feet (10.1 meters) long. (Illustration by Brian Cressman. Reproduced by permission.)

Reticulated pythons and people: People hunt this snake for its lovely skin, its meat, and for use in folk medicines. Some ranchers kill the snake because they are afraid it will eat their farm animals, while others destroy it because they worry it will eat their children or another person. In addition, the snakes are popular in the pet trade, although their large size soon makes them difficult to keep.

Conservation status: Reticulated pythons are not listed as endangered or threatened, but scientists know little about their numbers in the wild. ■

FOR MORE INFORMATION

Books

Barker, David G., and Tracy M. Barker. *Pythons of the World.* Vol. 1. *Australia.* Lakeside, CA: Advanced Vivarium Systems, Inc., 1994.

Brazaitis, P., and M. Watanabe. *Snakes of the World.* New York: Crescent Books, 1992.

Cleave, Andrew. *Snakes and Reptiles: A Portrait of the Animal World.* New York: Magna Books, 1994.

Cogger, Harold G. *Reptiles and Amphibians of Australia.* Sydney, Australia: Reed New Holland, 2000.

Greene, Harry W. *Snakes: The Evolution of Mystery in Nature.* Berkeley: University of California Press, 1997.

Lamar, W. *The World's Most Spectacular Reptiles and Amphibians.* Tampa, FL: World Publications, 1997.

Mattison, Chris. *Snake: The Essential Visual Guide to the World of Snakes.* New York: DK Publishing Inc., 1999.

McDonald, Mary Ann. *Pythons.* Minneapolis, MN: Capstone Press, 1996.

Minton, Sherman A., and Madge Rutherford Minton. *Giant Reptiles.* New York: Charles Scribner's Sons, 1973.

Murphy, John C., and Robert W. Henderson. *Tales of Giant Snakes: A Historical Natural History of Anacondas and Pythons.* Malabar, FL: Krieger Publishing Company, 1997.

O'Shea, Mark. *A Guide to the Snakes of Papua New Guinea.* Port Moresby, Papua, New Guinea: Independent Publishing Group, 1996.

Pope, Clifford Millhouse. *The Giant Snakes: The Natural History of the Boa Constrictor, the Anaconda, and the Largest Pythons, Including Comparative Facts About Other Snakes and Basic Information on Reptiles in General.* New York: Alfred A. Knopf, 1961.

Torr, Geordie. *Pythons of Australia: A Natural History.* Sydney, Australia: University of New South Wales Press, 2000.

Web sites

"Boas and Pythons." Singapore Zoological Gardens. http://www.szgdocent.org/cc/c-boa.htm (accessed on September 17, 2004).

"Green Tree Python." WhoZoo. http://www.whozoo.org/Intro98/jennglaz/jennglaz21.htm (accessed on September 17, 2004).

"Indian Python." Bagheera in the Wild. http://www.bagheera.com/inthewild/van_anim_python.htm (accessed on September 17, 2004).

"Pythons, Boas, and Anacondas: What's the Difference?" San Diego Zoo. http://www.sandiegozoo.org/animalbytes/t-python.html (accessed on September 20, 2004).

"Royal Python." Canadian Museum of Nature. http://www.nature.ca/notebooks/english/python.htm (accessed on September 17, 2004).

SPLITJAW SNAKE
Bolyeriidae

Class: Reptilia
Order: Squamata
Suborder: Serpentes
Family: Bolyeriidae
One species Splitjawsnake
(*Casarea dussumieri*)

phylum

class

subclass

order

monotypic order

suborder

▲ **family**

PHYSICAL CHARACTERISTICS

The splitjaw snake has an upper jaw bone split into front and back halves that are hinged together at a point just below the eye. With this unusual split in the jaw, the bone holding the upper teeth in the front of the mouth can bend up and down, while the bone holding the back teeth can stay in place. No other bird, mammal, reptile, amphibian, or fish has such a strangely jointed jaw. For many years, this snake was considered to be a member of the boa family, but its odd jaw was so unusual that scientists felt it should be in its own family. Despite its listing in its own family, the splitjaw snakes often go by common names that still include the word "boa."

Two members of this family existed in the 20th century, but only one has survived to enter the 21st century. The smooth-scaled splitjaw, also known as the smooth-scaled Round Island boa, is now believed to be extinct. The other species, the keel-scaled splitjaw, still exists today. The main difference between the two snakes is the presence or absence of small ridges, or keels, on the scales. Only the keel-scaled splitjaw has the ridges. In the splitjaws, as in other snakes, the ridges make the skin look a bit dull. Smooth scales, on the other hand, usually give snakes a shiny appearance.

The keel-scaled splitjaw is a thin snake with six-sided, or hexagonal (HEHK-SAE-guh-nuhl), scales running down its back. In many snake species, the back scales overlap, but the splitjaw's back scales barely touch each other, if at all. The snake has a long tail that makes up at least one-quarter of its entire body length. In snakes, the tail begins at the vent, a slitlike opening on the belly side. Its head is wider and flatter than the neck and is quite long, with an often noticeable black stripe behind the eye. Sometimes a white stripe lies alongside the black face stripe. The snake has a catlike pupil, but since its eye color is quite dark, the pupil is usually difficult to see. The upper body is light-to-dark brown, and the cream-colored belly is speckled with brown.

Some snake species have bits and pieces of leftover hip bones. In humans and other walking animals, the hip bones link to the leg bones, but since snakes have no legs, they do not need them. In splitjaws, no bits of hip bone remain. Adult keel-scaled splitjaws generally reach about 4 feet (1.3 meters) in length.

GEOGRAPHIC RANGE

Also known as the Round Island casarea boa, the keel-scaled splitjaw lives only on Round Island, which is located in the Indian Ocean east of Madagascar and just northwest of the island of Mauritius. At one time, this snake made its home on other small islands near Round Island and on the much-larger Mauritius, but now they live on just the one island. Round Island covers only 374 acres (151 hectares) and was created from lava ejected from a volcano. In the 1960s and 1970s, Round Island also had another species of splitjaw. During that period, observers on the island discovered a smooth-scaled splitjaw and watched the snake over a two-decade period. They were able to identify the snake from sighting to sighting by a distinctive scar on its body. They saw that lone snake on Round Island for the last time in 1975, and no one has ever seen a smooth-scaled splitjaw again. The discovery of the living snake was quite fortunate, because scientists would otherwise have never known of this species. While fossils of many other living and extinct snake species have been found, no one has ever found and identified a fossil from the smooth-scaled splitjaw.

HABITAT

The keel-scaled splitjaw prefers to live in the lush palm-covered rainforest of Round Island. Because much of the rainforest is now gone, however, the snake is surviving among stumps, scraggly bushes, and what few areas of thick forest it can find. The snake stays underground much of the time and therefore relies on proper soil conditions. Unfortunately, humans introduced animals, such as rabbits and goats, to the island. These animals eat plants and have completely wiped out many of the plants native to Round Island. Without the plants and their roots to hold the soil in place, rain can wash away and wind can blow away the soil that makes up the snake's habitat. Now, scientists estimate that 90 percent of the soil has disappeared.

DIET

A picky eater, the keel-scaled splitjaw snake eats little other than lizards, especially the day gecko and two types of skink. The splitjaw catches the slender and often-quick lizards during the day by remaining motionless and waiting for a lizard to accidentally come too close. The snake then strikes out and grabs the passing lizard. At night the splitjaw tries a different method. It hunts down the lizards using its senses of smell and sight. While holding most of its body close to the ground, the snake raises up its head a few inches (6 centimeters or so) and flicks its tongue. The tongue picks up scent chemicals in the air. It then slowly sneaks up on the lizard by slithering forward almost in a straight line, and when it gets near enough, strikes out to grab the animal.

BEHAVIOR AND REPRODUCTION

The keel-scaled splitjaw snake is mainly active at night, although it does do some hunting during the day. It usually stays on or under the ground, probably spending a good deal of its time in small moist tunnels, or burrows, which provide a safe hiding place. Splitjaw snakes will also climb up shrubs and tree limbs, sometimes reaching heights of 8 feet (2.5 meters). Scientists knew very little about the reproduction of this species until the Jersey Wildlife Preservation Trust, a group in the United Kingdom that tries to save endangered animals by breeding them in captivity, were able to get two captive snakes to mate successfully

ISLAND SNAKES

How do snakes, such as the keel-scaled splitjaw, get to islands? Although most people do not consider snakes to be swimmers, many of them can swim quite well for at least short distances. This explains how they reach islands close to shore, but sometimes snakes are found on islands far out in the ocean. In this case, some of them may have floated by climbing onto a large branch that was broken off a coastline tree and fell into the surf, or possibly they may have stowed away on a boat or a plane and slithered on shore after landing on the island. Another possibility is that a bird snatched up a snake on the mainland and held it in its claws to kill and eat later, only to accidentally drop it when it was flying over an island. Even though snakes can reach islands in many ways, some islands still have few, if any, of these animals. For example, only one species of land-living snake occurs on Hawaii. The snake, called the Brahminy blind snake, came to Hawaii from Asia probably in a shipping carton.

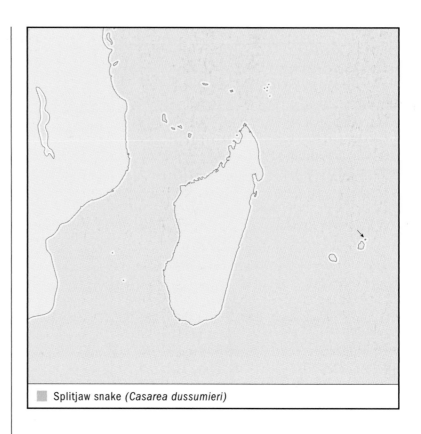

Splitjaw snake (*Casarea dussumieri*)

in 1982. The female laid eggs. Since then, other female keel-scaled splitjaws have laid eggs, too. No one has observed the snakes mating in the wild, but in captivity, they seem to mate most successfully from March to July and lay eggs from May to October. A female typically lays three to eleven soft-shelled eggs at a time, possibly laying them in a hidden spot, such as within a pile of leaves or inside a hollow tree trunk. Females may stay with the eggs for a while. When they hatch in about three months, the young are bright orange.

SPLITJAW SNAKES AND PEOPLE

People rarely see this snake in the wild.

CONSERVATION STATUS

The World Conservation Union (IUCN) and the U.S. Fish and Wildlife Service consider the Round Island casarea split-jaw to be Endangered, or facing a very high risk of extinction in the wild throughout all or a significant portion of its range. It once lived on the nearby and much larger Mauritus Island,

The splitjaw snake has an upper jaw bone split into front and back halves that are hinged together at a point just below the eye. (Illustration by Marguette Dongvillo. Reproduced by permission.)

but habitat loss, combined with the presence of non-native species, wiped out the splitjaws. On Round Island, the snakes had to survive the loss of the rainforest. In the 1970s, people became aware of the problems faced by the snakes and other animals on Round Island and set out to remove the non-native goats and rabbits that were eating the native plants, and therefore destroying the soil conditions needed by the snake. Now, to protect the rainforest further, only scientists and conservationists are allowed to visit Round Island. Plans are under way to remove non-native animals from a few other nearby small islands where the splitjaws once lived and possibly release some captive-bred splitjaws there. The hope is that the snakes will survive to breed and produce a wild population.

The U.S. Fish and Wildlife Service lists the smooth-scaled splitjaw as Endangered, but the World Conservation Union (IUCN) lists it as Extinct. No one has seen that species, also known as the Round Island bolyeria boa, since 1975.

FOR MORE INFORMATION

Books

Burnie, David, and Don Wilson, eds. *The Definitive Visual Guide to the World's Wildlife.* New York: DK Publishing, 2001. Page 379.

Day, David. *The Doomsday Book of Animals.* London: London Editions Limited, 1981.

Greene, Harry W. *Snakes: The Evolution of Mystery in Nature.* Berkeley: University of California Press, 1997.

Web sites

"*Round Island Keel-Scaled Boa* (Casarea dussumieri)." http://www .arkive.org/species/GES/reptiles/Casarea_dussumieri/more_info.html (accessed on September 8, 2004).

PHYSICAL CHARACTERISTICS

The woodsnakes and spinejaw snakes are small-to-medium-sized snakes that resemble boas. Colors range from gray to brown, and most have faint blotches or stripes. Some have smooth scales, and others have scales with ridges, or keels. Among those with smooth scales, the Oaxacan dwarf boa has scales that shine different colors depending on how the light hits them. Scales that do this are known as iridescent (IH-rih-DEH-sent). On the other hand, some members of this family have dull-looking scales with noticeable keels. The Cuban black and white dwarf boa even has scales that change color from darker during the daytime to lighter at night.

The smallest member of this family is the Cuban dusky trope, which reaches at most 12 inches (30 centimeters) long. The largest is the dusky dwarf boa, which can grow to 41 inches (104 centimeters) in length.

Some people believe that this family should be split in two with one keeping the name Tropidophiidae and the other falling under a new family called Ungaliophiidae. Occasionally, some books will place these snakes under the family Boidae, but although some have the common name of dwarf boas, they are not actually boas.

GEOGRAPHIC RANGE

They are found from Brazil to Mexico and in the West Indies. Some species are found in both Malaysia and Borneo.

phylum

class

subclass

order

monotypic order

suborder

▲ **family**

HABITAT

Different members of this family may prefer dry and open, shrubby forests; rainforests; the rocky sides of hills, as well as cliffs; farm fields; and even caves. Usually, they try to find a spot within the habitat that has conditions falling about halfway between wet and dry. Only two species make their homes high in mountains. Several species within this family are so rarely seen that they are only known by their scientific names.

DIET

Much of the information about the diet of these snakes comes from captive snakes rather than those in the wild. The West Indian species of the genus *Tropidophis* eat anoles, which are small, long-tailed lizards. Species in the genus *Exiliboa* feed on small salamanders and on frog eggs, while those in the genus *Trachyboa* make both fishes and amphibians part of their diet. Amphibians include such animals as salamanders and frogs. The dusky dwarf boa, which is the largest member of the family, will eat small mammals and birds. In captivity, many larger snakes in this group will eat baby mice.

BEHAVIOR AND REPRODUCTION

The snakes spend a good deal of time actively, but slowly, slithering through their habitat, apparently on the hunt for food. Scientists suspect that they also find hiding places, where they remain still and wait for the meal to come to them. This tactic, called ambush, is very effective for snakes like these that blend into the background very well. Most of the woodsnakes and spinejaw snakes live on the ground, but a few will also climb a few feet into trees or shrubs. The bromeliad woodsnakes are the best climbers in the family and will slink into plants, known as bromeliads (broh-MEE-lee-ads), that grow on the trunks and branches of tall trees.

Most of the woodsnakes and spinejaw snakes are active mainly at night, but they also come out during the day to sunbathe, or bask. When they feel threatened, the majority of the species will roll their bodies into a ball, rather than strike and bite as many other snakes do. Members of the genus *Trachyboa* coil into a flat disk instead of a ball, burying the head in the center of the disk. If an attacking animal, or predator (PREH-duh-ter), bites at a woodsnake, a bad-smelling material may ooze out of the snake's vent, a slitlike opening on the belly side of the animal. The odor is sometimes enough to cause the predator to leave. Only rarely will the snake bite back at an attacking animal. Some species in the genus *Tropidophis* have a rather unusual way of protecting themselves from predators. If a predator bothers them enough, they will begin to bleed from the mouth, nostrils, and eyes. Because the bleeding, or hemorrhaging (HEHM-rihj-ing), can start automatically—even though the snake has no injury—it is called autohemorrhaging (aw-toe-HEHM-rihj-ing).

Female woodsnakes and spinejaw snakes give birth to baby snakes, instead of eggs. Few people have studied this snake, so little additional information is available about their reproduction or behavior.

WOODSNAKES, SPINEJAW SNAKES, AND PEOPLE

Some are occasionally captured for the pet trade, but for the most part, people have little if any contact with these snakes.

CONSERVATION STATUS

This species is not listed as endangered or threatened. One species, the Navassa woodsnake, was noted as extinct in the 1990s, likely due to changes in its habitat and deaths from mongoose attacks. A mongoose is a ferretlike, meat-eating animal that is an excellent hunter.

■ Southern bromeliad woodsnake (*Ungaliophis panamensis*)

SOUTHERN BROMELIAD WOODSNAKE
Ungaliophis panamensis

Physical characteristics: Also known as the bromeliad boa, bromeliad dwarf boa, and banana boa, the southern bromeliad wood-snake is a thin, light gray or tan snake with black triangular marks on its back. It has smooth scales along its body with one large scale on top of its snout. Adults reach about 30 inches (76 centimeters) in length.

Geographic range: They live in Costa Rica, Nicaragua, and Panama in Central America and also in Colombia in northern South America.

Habitat: It lives in a variety of forests, except those of the mountains, often crawling among the plants that grow on the upper branches and high up in the trunks of trees. It also spends considerable time on the ground.

Diet: In captivity, southern bromeliad wood-snakes will eat lizards or rodents, although young snakes typically will only eat lizards. Scientists know little about their diet in the wild, but it probably includes lizards and frogs.

Behavior and reproduction: A mild-mannered snake, this species does not bite human handlers. Even when threatened, it will not bite and instead simply coils into a ball to wait for the danger to pass. It has another defense, however, which it will use if it feels particularly frightened. That defense is an ooze that seeps from its vent and has a strong enough smell to scare off most attackers. Females do not lay eggs and instead have baby snakes. The young are about 6 inches (15 centimeters) long at birth. Scientists know little else about this snake's behavior or reproduction.

Southern bromeliad woodsnakes and people: People rarely see this snake in the wild or in pet stores.

Conservation status: Scientists know so little about this snake, including how many of them live in the wild, that they cannot make any statements about its conservation status.

ESD©2003

Much of the information about southern bromeliad woodsnakes comes from captive snakes rather than those in the wild. (Illustration by Emily Damstra. Reproduced by permission.)

FOR MORE INFORMATION

Books

Brazaitis, P., and M. Watanabe. *Snakes of the World.* New York: Crescent Books, 1992.

Burnie, David, and Don Wilson, eds. *The Definitive Visual Guide to the World's Wildlife.* New York: DK Publishing, 2001.

Crother, Brian I., ed. *Caribbean Amphibians and Reptiles.* San Diego: Academic Press, 1999.

Duellman, William E., ed. *The South American Herpetofauna: Its Origin, Evolution and Dispersal.* Monograph of the Museum of Natural History, Number 7. Lawrence: The University of Kansas, 1979.

Greene, Harry W. *Snakes: The Evolution of Mystery in Nature.* Berkeley: University of California Press, 1997.

Lamar, W. *The World's Most Spectacular Reptiles and Amphibians.* Tampa, FL: World Publications, 1997.

McDiarmid, Roy W., Jonathan A. Campbell, and T'Shaka A. Touré. *Snake Species of the World.* Washington, DC: The Herpetologists' League, 1999.

Schwartz, Albert, and Robert W. Henderson. *Amphibians and Reptiles of the West Indies.* Gainesville: University of Florida Press, 1991.

Tolson, P. J., and R. W. Henderson. *The Natural History of West Indian Boas.* Taunton: R & A Publishing Limited, 1993.

Zug, G. R., L. J. Vitt, and J. P. Caldwell. *Herpetology.* 5th ed. San Diego: Academic Press, 2001.

Web sites

"Talking Taino: Lizards and Snakes." Times of the Islands. Summer 2004. http://www.timespub.tc/Natural%20History/Archive/Summer2003/ttsnake.htm (accessed on September 15, 2004).

FILE SNAKES
Acrochordidae

Class: Reptilia

Order: Squamata

Family: Acrochordidae

Number of species: 3 species

phylum

class

subclass

order

monotypic order

suborder

▲ **family**

PHYSICAL CHARACTERISTICS

Also known as wart snakes or elephant-trunk snakes, the file snakes have baggy skin that lies in loose folds. The skin is covered with tiny scales and small, bristly outgrowths that make the skin seem quite rough. This rough skin looks rather like the surface of a file, and some say it also looks as if it is covered with small warts; it is the appearance of their skin that gives them the common name "file" snakes. Although for many years people thought that the little file snake was venomous (VEH-nuh-mus), or poisonous, and dangerous to humans, scientists now know that none of the three file snake species, or types, has a bite that can harm a person.

File snakes spend nearly their entire lives in the water. A file snake has both its eyes and its nostrils, or nose holes, located on the top of its short head, so it can breathe the air and see above the water surface while the rest of the body remains underwater. The nostrils also have little valves, or flaps, that can close up when the snake dips completely below the water's surface. The tail is somewhat flattened from side to side and helps the snake swim. Male and female file snakes look very much alike, except that the females have slightly larger heads, thicker bodies, and shorter tails. The tail on a snake is the part of the body that extends back from a slit on the belly. File snakes range in length from about 20 to 76 inches (0.5 to 2 meters). The little file snake is the smallest member of the family, averaging 20 to 28 inches (51 to 71 centimeters) in length but sometimes reaching 40 inches (1 meter). The Arafura file snake grows to

about 67 inches (1.7 meters), and the Java file snake grows to 76 inches (2 meters).

GEOGRAPHIC RANGE

The file snakes live from India to Southeast Asia and Australia. They inhabit northern Australia, the Solomon Islands east of New Guinea, Malaysia, and Indonesia.

HABITAT

The file snakes usually live in warm, shallow waters. The Arafura and Java file snakes live in freshwater streams; lagoons, or shallow bodies of saltwater near the sea; and rivers. In the dry season, the Arafura file snake is also found in billabongs (BILL-uh-bongs), which are dried-up streambeds. During the rainy season, it will slither into flooded grasslands. The Java file snake, on the other hand, occasionally swims into the salty ocean water for short periods of time. Little file snakes can live in both freshwater and saltwater areas, from the ocean to swamps near the coastline and to inland rivers, sometimes up to 6 miles (9.6 kilometers) out to sea and in water up to 66 feet (20 meters) deep. Little file snakes have salt glands, small groups of cells that may help them control the amount of salt in their bodies. Salt glands are also seen in many other animals that live in salty waters. Scientists have not studied this gland in detail, however, so they are unsure how important it is to the snake's survival in saltwater.

DIET

The three file snake species eat mostly fishes, and they do not seem to care whether the meal is alive or dead when they find it. The little file snake also eats crustaceans (krus-TAY-shuns). Crustaceans include shelled animals, such as shrimp and crayfish. The Java file snake adds freshwater eels to its diet of mainly catfishes. The Arafura file snake can eat very large fishes. According to one report, a snake that measured 44.5 inches (113 centimeters) in length ate a 19-inch-long (48-centimeter-long) fish—nearly half the snake's size—in just two minutes.

BEHAVIOR AND REPRODUCTION

The file snakes rarely leave the water, but they occasionally move from one body of water to another during the wet and dry seasons or when ocean water levels rise and fall due to the tides. During the daytime, they stay among roots, in holes in the muddy water bottom, or in other hiding places and come out to hunt for food at night. Using the bristles in the outgrowths on their skin, file snakes can sense changes in the murky, or dark, water, which helps locate animals that they might otherwise be unable to see. To hunt, a file snake either will strike out and grasp a passing fish with its mouth or will quickly wrap its body around the fish and hold it until the snake can reach around with its head to bite and eat the fish. Unlike constrictor (kun-STRIK-tuhr) snakes that wrap around and squeeze their prey to death before eating it, the file snake coils around the prey only to hold it temporarily until it can quickly gulp it down. Although they can swim quite well, adults usually move slowly along the bottom. Scientists know very little about the behavior of young file snakes.

Java and little file snakes have young every other year, and Arafura file snakes have young even less often. All of the three species lay eggs, probably from the middle of the wet season to late in the wet season. The little file snake has about five eggs at a time, the Arafura file snake has about seventeen, and the Java file snake lays an average of twenty-six eggs. At least among the Arafura file snakes, larger females have a larger number of young.

FILE SNAKES AND PEOPLE

Some people collect file snakes as food and for their skin, which is used for leather. Since the snake reproduces only once every two years, or even less often, such collecting over the years could lead to dangerous drops in the numbers of snakes. People only rarely collect file snakes for the pet trade.

CONSERVATION STATUS

File snakes are not considered threatened, but some populations may have low numbers. Habitat loss, as well as habitat damage from water pollution, or dirtying and poisoning of water, may hurt their ability to survive into the future. In areas with large fish populations, however, file snakes can become very numerous. Scientists have counted 100 or more Arafura file snakes on every 2 acres (0.8 hectare) of some Australian billabongs.

PHYSICAL CHARACTERISTICS

Vipers and pitvipers are mainly known for the pair of short hollow fangs that usually lie flat in the upper jaw but swing down when the snake opens its mouth to inject its venom. The members of this family are typically rather thick snakes with large triangular-shaped heads, usually catlike eye pupils, and short tails. The tail in a snake is the part of the body behind the vent, a slitlike opening on the belly side of the animal. Those snakes that spend much of their time climbing among shrubs and trees have longer tails. Some vipers and pitvipers have zigzag, diamond-shaped, or other patterns on their backs, but for the most part, vipers and pitvipers have no showy colors and instead simply blend into the background, which often makes them difficult to spot.

The pitvipers are unusual because each has a rattle on the end of the tail and a small but deep pit on either side of the face. The rattle is made of little segments of fingernail-like material that make a noise when they knock against one another. The snake gets a new segment every time it sheds, but the oldest segments frequently fall off. The pits on the snake's face are sensitive to temperature, so the pitvipers have infrared (IN-fruh-red) vision, which is the ability to detect, or to "see," heat.

Vipers and pitvipers come in different sizes. The smallest member of the family is the dwarf puff adder, which grows to about 12 inches (30.5 centimeters). The largest are some of the pitvipers, which reach 11.8 feet (3.6 meters) in length.

GEOGRAPHIC RANGE

Vipers and pitvipers are found in North, Central, and South America and in Africa, Europe, and Asia.

HABITAT

Most members of this family live on land, but some, such as the cottonmouth, spend a good part of their time in the water. Vipers and pitvipers make their homes in warm tropical climates and in cooler temperate climates that have distinct seasons, including cold winters. Temperate species often move from one habitat to another during the spring, summer, and fall and then hibernate through the winter. For example, North America's eastern massasauga rattlesnake spends the early spring near wetlands, moves into drier nearby fields for the hot summer months, and hibernates back near the water in underground burrows made by crayfish or small mammals. During hibernation (high-bur-NAY-shun), the animal enters a state of deep sleep that helps it to survive the frigid weather.

DIET

Vipers and pitvipers eat mice, rats, and lizards, but they will also feed on birds, frogs, and other animals. A few of the smallest species eat locusts, a type of grasshopper.

Vipers and pitvipers are predators (PREH-dih-ters) and use their venom when hunting prey or sometimes when defending themselves. The venom attacks the blood system of the prey, producing burning pain and other symptoms, and later stopping the heart. A few vipers and pitvipers have venom that also attacks the nervous system. Some species slowly slither along looking for prey animals, but others rely on their camouflage-like colors to hide them until an unsuspecting animal happens by. In either case, the snake lashes out at the prey animal with great speed, opening its mouth to swing down its fangs and biting the animal to inject the venom—all in the blink of an eye. The prey never even sees the snake until it is too late.

BEHAVIOR AND REPRODUCTION

The defense behaviors of the vipers and pitvipers are perhaps their best-known feature. The snakes coil up into a flat spiral with the head curved up from the middle of the coil. Some also hiss, jerk forward with the head, rattle the tail, or blow up the

body, which makes the snake look larger. Each of the behaviors may be enough to scare off a predator. Many of the warmer climate species remain active all year long, but the temperate species may hibernate for many weeks. Those living high up in the mountains and other places with especially cold winters typically hibernate for several, sometimes up to eight, months a year.

Males mate every year in the spring or fall, sometimes wrestling with other males over the chance to mate with a female. Females, especially those in colder climates, often skip a year or more between matings. The females of most species produce eggs, but these hatch inside her body so that she gives birth to baby snakes. A few species, such as the night adders, lay eggs instead. Recent research suggests that some mothers may linger around the young for a few days, possibly providing some protection against predators that may hunt them for food.

VIPERS, PITVIPERS, AND PEOPLE

While viper and pitviper bites of humans are quite rare, they do occur often enough and cause enough deaths to be a concern in some areas. For this reason, people often kill vipers and pitvipers, along with any other snakes that remotely resemble them. In addition, people hunt and kill these snakes to use in medicines.

CONSERVATION STATUS

According to the World Conservation Union (IUCN), seven species are Critically Endangered; four species are Endangered; seven species are Vulnerable, and one species is listed as Data Deficient. The Critically Endangered species face an extremely high risk of extinction in the wild, while the Endangered species face a very high risk, and the Vulnerable face a high risk. Scientists have too little information on those noted as Data Deficient to make a judgment about the threat of extinction. The U.S. Fish and Wildlife Service lists one U.S. and one foreign species as Threatened or likely to become endangered in the foreseeable future, and one foreign species as Endangered or in danger of extinction throughout all or a significant portion of its range. Overall, the loss of habitat and outright killing of the snakes by humans are the greatest risks the snakes face.

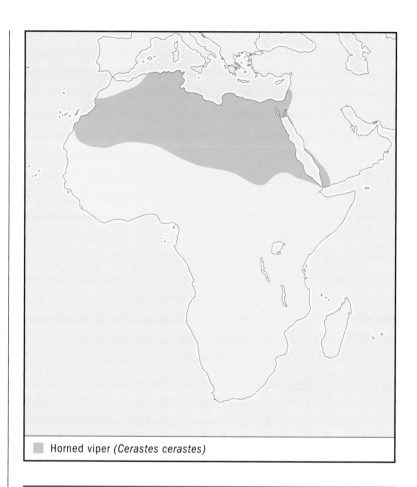

Horned viper (*Cerastes cerastes*)

HORNED VIPER
Cerastes cerastes

Physical characteristics: A thick snake with a short tail, the horned viper has a triangle-shaped head and a long scale over each eye that pokes up like a horn. Some individuals have a ridge over their eyes instead of the two tall horns. They have brown blotches down a gray, yellow- or red-tinged back, and the back and head scales have ridges, or keels. Adults are quite small, usually growing to just 11.8 to 23.6 inches (30 to 60 centimeters), although a few reach 2.8 feet (85 centimeters).

Geographic range: Horned vipers are found in northern Africa and the eastern Sinai.

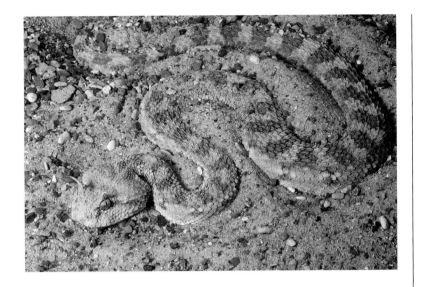

Unlike most snakes, the horned viper can dig into the ground and bury itself. It waits, often with just its horns above the ground, for a prey animal to walk nearby and then strikes and bites the animal. (©Gregory G. Dimijian/Photo Researchers, Inc.)

Habitat: This species lives mostly in sandy areas, sometimes marked with stones and rocks.

Diet: They eat other animals of sandy habitats. These may include small mammals, lizards, and birds.

Behavior and reproduction: This snake is active at night. It hides during the day beneath rocks or in underground tunnels made by other animals. Unlike most snakes, the horned viper can dig into the ground and bury itself. It waits, often with just its horns above the ground, for a prey animal to walk nearby and then strikes and bites the animal. When it slithers, the horned viper slides sideways across the sand in what is known as sidewinding. This is an egg-laying snake, and the females lay between ten and twenty-three eggs at a time.

Horned vipers and people: Since it hides during the day, people rarely see the horned viper. It does, however, sometimes bite people, but the bites are not thought to be that dangerous.

Conservation status: This species is not considered endangered or threatened. ■

Cottonmouth (*Agkistrodon piscivorus*)

COTTONMOUTH
Agkistrodon piscivorus

Physical characteristics: The cottonmouth gets its common name from the white, cottonlike color inside its mouth. Also known as the water moccasin, it is a large thick snake. Younger adults have brown or reddish bands on a yellowish background, while older individuals are usually all brown, greenish brown, or black. Juveniles have tails that are tipped with yellow or green. In the wild, adults may reach 5.9 feet (1.8 meters) in length and weigh 10 pounds (4.6 kilograms).

Geographic range: They are found in the southeastern quarter of the United States.

Habitat: The cottonmouth spends most of its time in or near the water, although it will sometimes crawl some distance onto land.

The cottonmouth spends most of its time in or near the water, although it will sometimes crawl some distance onto land. (Joe McDonald/Bruce Coleman Inc. Reproduced by permission.)

Diet: Cottonmouths will eat almost any animals they find. This includes birds, eggs, living and sometimes dead fishes, frogs, small alligators and turtles, snakes and other cottonmouths, and mammals.

Behavior and reproduction: Cottonmouths spend much of their time coiled up and out in the open. They hunt for food by swimming or slithering around looking for it or by staying still and waiting for the prey to mistakenly come a little too close. When they feel threatened, cottonmouths will strike and bite, but usually they remain motionless until the threat passes. Snakes that live in warmer areas are active all year, but those living in colder areas hibernate during the winter. During mating season, males sometimes fight one another for the chance to mate with a female. Females give birth to baby snakes instead of eggs in August or September. They have up to sixteen young at a time.

Cottonmouths and people: Although most cottonmouths are content to leave people alone, bites do occur. The venom is dangerous to humans and can be fatal. Humans also pose a great risk to the snakes by draining wetlands and otherwise destroying their habitat and also by killing the snakes out of fear.

Conservation status: This species is not considered endangered or threatened. ■

Timber rattlesnake (*Crotalus horridus*)

TIMBER RATTLESNAKE
Crotalus horridus

Physical characteristics: The timber rattlesnake is a thick snake, often with dark, sometimes V-shaped blotches running down a black, dark or light brown, yellowish, or gray back. It has a large triangle-shaped head at one end and a black rattle-tipped tail at the other. Adults often reach nearly 5 feet (1.5 meters) in length, and some grow to more than 6 feet (1.8 meters).

Geographic range: They are found in much of the eastern United States.

Habitat: Timber rattlesnakes prefer rocky ledges on hills, although they travel into nearby forests, especially in the warmer months.

Diet: They have only six to twenty meals a year, but when they do eat, they hunt for mammals, and sometimes birds, lizards, frogs, insects, and other snakes.

Behavior and reproduction: Timber rattlesnakes spend much of their time either sunbathing, also known as basking, or sitting still to wait for their next meal to wander within striking distance. In the winter, this snake hibernates either alone or in groups. Females only mate once every two, three, or four years, giving birth to between three and nineteen live baby snakes at a time. The young snakes must reach four to nine years old before they can mate and have their own young.

Timber rattlesnakes and people: Bites to humans are uncommon but can be dangerous, although rarely fatal.

Conservation status: This species is not considered endangered or threatened. ■

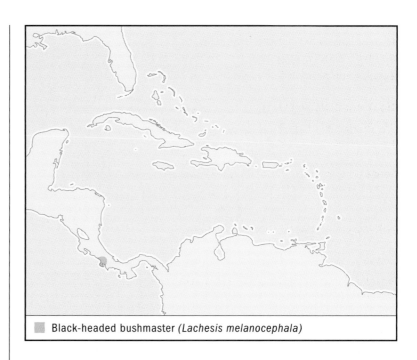

Black-headed bushmaster (*Lachesis melanocephala*)

BLACK-HEADED BUSHMASTER
Lachesis melanocephala

Physical characteristics: As its name says, the top of the black-headed bushmaster's head is black. The back of this large snake has black diamond-shaped blotches on a dark or light brown or yellowish background. Adults often reach 6.6 feet (2 meters) in length but can grow to 7.9 feet (2.4 meters).

Geographic range: They are found in Costa Rica, possibly reaching into Panama.

Habitat: This species lives in wet or moist forests in valleys and other low places.

Diet: The black-headed bushmaster apparently eats mainly mammals.

Behavior and reproduction: A land-living snake, the black-headed bushmaster remains still much of the time, waiting for animals to wander by. If it is hungry, it will strike out and bite the passing animal. When it is not hunting, it often stays in underground tunnels made by other animals. If threatened, it may shake its tail. This is an egg-laying species, and females lay up to sixteen eggs. Unlike many reptiles, the female remains with her eggs until they hatch.

Black-headed bushmasters and people: If they are left untreated, humans bitten by this snake may die.

Conservation status: This species is not considered endangered or threatened. ∎

Black-headed bushmaster adults often reach 6.6 feet (2 meters) in length but can grow to 7.9 feet (2.4 meters). (Illustration by Dan Erickson. Reproduced by permission.)

FOR MORE INFORMATION

Books

Brazaitis, Peter, and Myrna E. Watanabe. *Snakes of the World.* New York: Crescent Books, 1992.

Campbell, Jonathan A., and Edmund D. Brodie Jr. *Biology of the Pitvipers.* Tyler, TX: Selva, 1992.

Campbell, Jonathan A., and William W. Lamar. *The Venomous Reptiles of Latin America.* Ithaca, NY: Cornell University Press, 1989.

Campbell, Jonathan A., and William W. Lamar. *The Venomous Reptiles of the Western Hemisphere.* Ithaca, NY: Cornell University Press, 2003.

Ernst, Carl H. *Venomous Reptiles of North America.* Washington, DC: Smithsonian Institution Press, 1992.

Gloyd, Howard K., and Roger Conant. "Snakes of the *Agkistrodon* Complex: A Monographic Review." *Contributions to Herpetology, Vol. 6.* Oxford, OH: Society for the Study of Amphibians and Reptiles, 1990.

Harding, James. *Amphibians and Reptiles of the Great Lakes Region.* Ann Arbor, MI: University of Michigan Press, 1997.

Holman, J. Alan, and James Harding. *Michigan Snakes.* East Lansing, MI: Michigan State University Extension, 1989.

Jena, I. *Snakes of Medical Importance and Snake-bite Treatment.* New Delhi: Ashish Publishing House, 1985.

Lamar, W. *The World's Most Spectacular Reptiles and Amphibians.* Tampa, FL: World Publications, 1997.

Mallow, D., D. Ludwig, and G. Nilson. *True Vipers: Natural History and Toxinology of Old World Vipers.* Melbourne, FL: Krieger Publishing Company, 2003.

Nilson, G., and C. Andrén. "Evolution, Systematics and Biogeography of Palearctic Vipers." In *Venomous Snakes: Ecology, Evolution and Snakebite,* edited by R. S. Thorpe, W. Wüster, and A. Malhotra. Symposia of the Zoological Society of London. London: Oxford University Press, 1997.

Palmer, T. *Landscape with Reptile: Rattlesnakes in an Urban World.* New York: Ticknor and Fields, 1992.

Schuett, Gordon W., Mats Höggren, Michael E. Douglas, and Harry W. Greene, eds. *Biology of the Vipers.* Eagle Mountain, UT: Eagle Mountain Publishing, 2002.

Spawls, S., and B. Branch. *The Dangerous Snakes of Africa.* Sanibel Island, FL: Ralph Curtis Books, 1995.

family

CHAPTER

PHYSICAL CHARACTERISTICS

The African burrowing snakes have small heads, rounded at the front. Their heads are no larger in diameter than their necks. Only the quill-snouted snake has a head that comes to a point. The members of this family have small, sometimes very tiny, eyes with round pupils. Most have fangs, or long, pointed teeth, at the rear of the mouth, but some have hollow fangs at the front of the mouth. These front fangs swing out to inject venom, or poison, into their prey, animals that they hunt for food, or their predators (PREH-duh-ters), the animals that hunt them for food.

These small to medium-sized snakes are long and thin; adults range in length from about 12 to 40 inches (30 to 102 centimeters), from head to tail tip. Most are black or brown with a different-colored ring around the neck. A few have bright stripes. All have smooth scales, instead of the ridged scales seen in many other snakes.

GEOGRAPHIC RANGE

Most African burrowing snakes live in the central and southern regions of Africa, known as sub-Saharan Africa, but a few make their homes in Israel or in Jordan.

HABITAT

Just as their name suggests, this group of snakes likes to live in burrows, or tunnels, underground. They are especially fond of sandy soils. Some like the damp soil of lowland forests, but others can live quite well in the drier sands of grasslands and areas that are almost desertlike.

phylum

class

subclass

order

monotypic order

suborder

▲ **family**

DIET

African burrowing snakes typically eat other animals that like to live underground. Depending on the species, or type, of snake, the meals may include lizards, blind snakes, worm lizards, centipedes (sen-tuh-PEEDS), and frogs. The larger African burrowing snakes will also eat rodents, a group of animals that includes mice. Some species will eat a variety of different animals, but some are very particular. One kind of quill-snouted snake, for example, eats only large worm lizards. Although scientists are unsure how the snakes successfully attack and kill such a large animal, they suspect that this snake stabs the lizard to death with its hard and pointed head. Other picky diners are the "centipede eaters," which rarely make a meal out of anything except the small, many-legged animals called centipedes. The snake grabs the centipede and chews it with its rear fangs to inject venom. When the venom knocks out or kills the centipede, the snake turns it around to swallow it head first.

BEHAVIOR AND REPRODUCTION

Also known as mole vipers or burrowing asps, members of this family are known best for their underground lifestyles. Some African burrowing snakes only crawl through tunnels that other animals make, but some can force their heads through loose sand and "dig" their own tunnels. Most of these snakes (except the burrowing asp) have fangs at the rear of the mouth, and so they must take a full bite to get any benefit from their fangs.

A burrowing asp, on the other hand, has two long, hollow fangs at the front of the mouth that it uses to inject venom into a prey animal or to protect itself from a predator. This unusual snake holds just one of its two backward-curving fangs outside its mouth and, keeping its mouth closed, stabs sideways and backward with its head to hook the bare fang into the prey or predator. This unusual backward-curved fang can make the snake quite dangerous to humans who mistakenly believe that they can safely hold the snake behind the head. With a quick backward flick of the head, the snake can force its fang into a human's hand. This unique venom-delivery system has given several other common names to the burrowing asp, including side-stabbing snake and stiletto snake. A stiletto is a type of thin, sharp knife.

During breeding time, many species come out of their underground tunnels to find mates. The females of all except one species of African burrowing snake lay eggs. Typically, the female will lay two to fifteen oblong-shaped eggs, either in moist soil or inside an old and unused termite nest. The eggs hatch in six to eight weeks into young snakes that are about 6 to 8 inches (15 to 20 centimeters) long. The exception is the Jackson's centipede eater, which gives birth to two or three live young that are about 4 inches (10 centimeters) long.

AFRICAN BURROWING SNAKES AND PEOPLE

Most African burrowing snakes are not dangerous to humans, but some have venom powerful enough to make people sick and sometimes kill them. Bites typically occur at night, when people accidentally step on a snake or turn over in bed and roll onto a snake that has crawled under the covers. For the most part, however, African burrowing snakes are gentle animals that rarely bite humans. The burrowing asps are different. When humans even slightly bother a burrowing asp, it will strike again and again.

CONSERVATION STATUS

A few species of African burrowing snake live in very small areas, but no species is endangered or threatened.

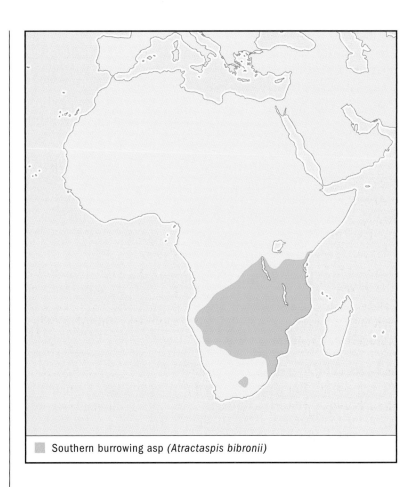

Southern burrowing asp (*Atractaspis bibronii*)

SPECIES ACCOUNT

SOUTHERN BURROWING ASP
Atractaspis bibronii

Physical characteristics: Also known as Bibron's burrowing asp or the side-stabbing snake, the southern burrowing asp has backward-curved fangs at the front of its mouth. This snake has a thick body, with smooth, purplish-brown to black scales down its back and, usually, a dark-gray belly. A few have dark blotches on a whitish to cream-colored belly. Females can reach 24.4 inches (62 centimeters) in length, and males can grow to about 26 inches (66 centimeters).

Geographic range: This snake is found in the southern half of Africa.

Habitat: These snakes spend much of their lives underground in savannas, flat plains covered with grass and a few trees. They also live in dry, nearly desert habitats and near the coast in thick, brushy areas.

Diet: The southern burrowing asp eats other reptiles, rodents, and frogs.

Behavior and reproduction: True to their name, these snakes can dig through the soil. Much of their digging is done to make hollow compartments under rocks. They usually remain underground, but sometimes they come to the surface at night after a rainstorm. They have an unusual smell, but scientists still are unsure if that smell has any purpose, such as attracting mates or scaring off attackers. In the summer female southern burrowing asps each lay four to eleven oblong eggs, which hatch into 6-inch-long (15-centimeter-long) young snakes.

Southern burrowing asps usually remain underground, but sometimes they come to the surface at night after a rainstorm. (Illustration by Bruce Worden. Reproduced by permission.)

Southern burrowing asps and people: When people and burrowing asps live in the same area, snakebites are somewhat common. A bite can lead to pain and swelling, but it will not kill humans.

Conservation status: This species is not endangered or threatened. ∎

FOR MORE INFORMATION

Books:

Branch, Bill. *Field Guide to Snakes and Other Reptiles of Southern Africa.* Sanibel Island, FL: Ralph Curtis Books, 1998.

Lovett, Sarah. *Extremely Weird Snakes.* Santa Fe, NM: John Muir Publications, 1999.

Mattison, Chris. *The Encyclopedia of Snakes.* New York: Facts on File, 1995.

Montgomery, Sy. *The Snake Scientist.* Boston: Houghton Mifflin, 2001.

Spawls, Stephen, and Bill Branch. *The Dangerous Snakes of Africa: Natural History, Species Directory, Venoms, and Snakebite.* Sanibel Island, FL: Ralph Curtis Books, 1995.

Spawls, Stephen, et al. *A Field Guide to the Reptiles of East Africa: Kenya, Tanzania, Uganda, Rwanda, and Burundi.* San Diego: Academic Press, 2002.

Web sites:

"Ecoviews: Africa Really Does Have Some Dangerous Snakes." University of Georgia Savannah River Ecology Laboratory. http://www.uga.edu/srelherp/ecoview/Eco16.htm (accessed on August 26, 2004).

COLUBRIDS

Colubridae

Class: Reptilia

Order: Squamata

Family: Colubridae

Number of species: 1,700 species

PHYSICAL CHARACTERISTICS

The colubrids (KAHL-yuh-bruhds) make up the largest group of snakes; they include almost 75 percent of all the world's snake species, or types of snakes. These snakes come in many sizes, shapes, and colors. Despite the many differences among the snakes in this family, colubrids share a few features. Most have wide scales on their bellies and, usually, nine large scales on the tops of their heads. Most colubrids also have glands, or groups of cells, behind each eye. These glands squeeze out a mixture of chemicals that, in some species, oozes through enlarged back teeth, known as rear fangs. When a colubrid bites down on a prey animal, this venom, or poison, trickles into the prey animal; the venom slows down, knocks out, or kills the animal, which the colubrid then eats. Unlike the cobras and vipers, whose fast-acting venom can knock out or kill an animal in moments, the colubrids produce venom that is not as strong and usually takes many minutes to work. The boomslangs and a few other species are exceptions to the rule; they have venom powerful enough to kill humans. Antivenin (an-tee-VEH-nuhn), a remedy that neutralizes, or makes ineffective, the poison of the snake, is available to treat the bites.

Colubrid snakes range widely in size, with some species growing to about 6 inches (15.2 centimeters) and others reaching 12 feet (3.7 meters) in length. Depending on the species, males may be larger than females, or females may be larger than males.

phylum

class

subclass

order

monotypic order

suborder

▲ **family**

GEOGRAPHIC RANGE

Colubrid snakes occur almost everywhere in the world. The only places they do not live are Antarctica; the far northern reaches of Europe, Asia, and North America; and central and western Australia.

HABITAT

The snakes in this family make their homes in many different places. Some spend most of their time underground, some climb into trees and shrubs, some slither about mostly on the ground, and others live mainly in water. Most of the water-living colubrids like freshwater habitats, but a few, like the crab-eating water snake, can live in saltier water. A particularly unusual colubrid is the Southeast Asian flying snake, which not only climbs trees but also soars from one tree branch to another. These snakes do not actually fly but instead flatten out their bodies and soar from a higher branch to a lower one.

DIET

Depending on the species, colubrids may eat mammals, lizards, baby turtles, frogs and toads, fishes, earthworms, scorpions, tarantulas, some insects, and any number of other animals that will fit in their mouths. Some colubrids will eat almost anything that comes their way. Others will eat only a handful of different food items, and a few are extremely picky about their meals. For example, the rainbow snake dines on eels and little else, and the egg eaters of Africa swallow only whole bird eggs. In some species, snakes that eat one type of prey as youngsters continue eating that type of prey into adulthood. Many common garter snakes that grow up eating earthworms, for example, stick to a mostly earthworm diet as adults.

BEHAVIOR AND REPRODUCTION

Scientists have not studied the activities of most of the 1,700 colubrid species in any detail, because many of them live underground or in trees, or else they have excellent camouflage (KA-mah-flahzh), a sort of disguise, which makes them difficult to watch. Scientists do, however, have a lot of information about the more common snakes and even some particularly odd types. The most obvious features of many colubrids are their defensive methods. Often, snakes make their bodies appear bigger to scare off attacking animals, known as predators (PREH-duh-ters). For instance, the false water cobras spread their necks into a hood, giving them the look of much larger snakes. Some colubrid snakes will open their mouths wide and might even strike and bite. Many, including the northern ribbon snake, give off bad-smelling substances to convince predators that they should leave them alone.

A wide variety of colubrid snakes find that the best way to keep away from predators is to move away as quickly as possible. Other snakes act like venomous (VEH-nuh-mus), or poisonous, species, or they have coloring that copycats the coloring of venomous species. For example, the scarlet kingsnake has no dangerous venom, but it looks very much like the venomous eastern coral snake, and the milk snake, that has no dangerous venom, will wiggle its tail just as a venomous rattlesnake does.

Many colubrids that live in cool climates, particularly those with very cold winters, will hibernate (HIGH-bur-nayt), or become inactive and sleep deeply, to help them survive the frigid (FRIH-juhd) weather. Although most snakes do not dig, they will use other animals' underground homes as places to hibernate. Snakes will also sometimes hibernate among tree roots; inside old, rotting tree stumps; or in any other protected spot they can find.

During mating season, which usually happens once a year, the males of many colubrid species will wrestle with one another. In these fights two snakes usually twist their bodies around each other while trying to tip over the opponent. The winner approaches the female to mate. In some species, the male flicks his tongue at the female and presses his head against the female's back before mating. Tongue flicking is also used in hunting. Snakes do not really have a sense of smell. When a snake flicks out its tongue, it picks up scent (SENT) chemicals from the air. The snake then presses its tongue against the roof of its mouth and "smells" the scent, or odor, in that way.

Most colubrid snakes lay eggs, but some females give birth to live snakes. Typically, the females lay eggs in a hole or tunnel in the ground or under some rotting leaves. The smaller

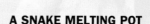

A SNAKE MELTING POT

When considering all of the snakes in the world, nearly three of every four species is a member of the family Colubridae. Scientists have been struggling for many years to decide for sure if all of these snakes should remain in one large family or be split up into several smaller families. For now, however, they are all in one large family that is divided into smaller groups, called subfamilies. Not everyone agrees on the arrangement of the snakes in these subfamilies or even on the number of subfamilies, however, so plenty of work is left to do.

species have fewer young than the larger species. Some of the smallest colubrids, such as the worm snakes, may lay only three eggs at a time, while larger species, like mud snakes, may lay more than thirty eggs. The diamond-backed water snake gives birth to nearly fifty live young at a time. For some species, the female's duties are complete as soon as she gives birth, but for others, the female will stay near her nest and protect her eggs.

COLUBRIDS AND PEOPLE

Humans are much more dangerous to colubrids than colubrids are to humans. People collect the snakes for pets or for food and, occasionally, for their skins, which are made into leather. For their part, most colubrids are of no danger to humans. Even those species with large or grooved rear teeth that can inject humans with mild venom typically do little more harm with their bites than to cause a bit of swelling at the bite spot. A few unusual species, including the boomslangs and twig snakes of Africa, have venom powerful enough to kill humans.

CONSERVATION STATUS

The World Conservation Union (IUCN) lists one species as Extinct, meaning that none is still alive. Six species are Critically Endangered, meaning that they face an extremely high risk of extinction in the wild, and seven are Endangered, meaning that they face a very high risk of extinction. Eight are considered Vulnerable, meaning that their risk of extinction is high, and four are Near Threatened, meaning that they may face the risk of becoming threatened with extinction in the near future. The U.S. Fish and Wildlife Service lists seven U.S. species and one foreign colubrid as Threatened.

The danger to most colubrid populations comes from the destruction of their habitat, or their preferred living areas, and their collection for the pet trade, food, or leather. While many species are finding it hard to survive, the brown tree snake is doing very well. This slender snake grows to 4.5 to 6.5 feet (1.4 to 2 meters) in length. It is native to Indonesia, New Guinea, Australia, and the Solomon Islands, but it seems to have hitched a ride on military ships during World War II to the Pacific island of Guam. Once there, it quickly adapted to its new home and has since hunted and eaten to extinction several species of the island's native birds and lizards.

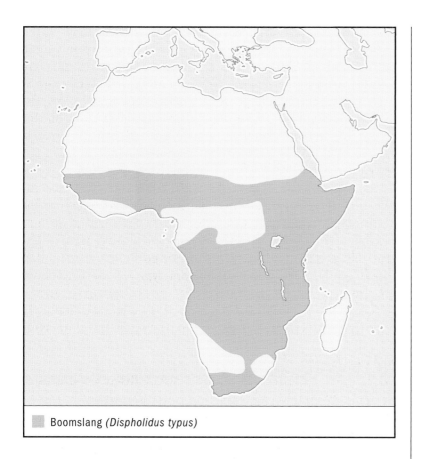

Boomslang *(Dispholidus typus)*

BOOMSLANG
Dispholidus typus

Physical characteristics: A long, thin snake, the boomslang comes in a number of colors, including green, reddish, and black with yellow spots inside each of the black scales. The belly is often a creamy color. The boomslang has a large head and big eyes. Adults are about 4 feet (1.2 meters) long.

Geographic range: The boomslang lives in the central and southern regions of Africa, which is known as sub-Saharan Africa.

Habitat: This snake spends most of its time crawling among the branches of trees and shrubs in forests and grasslands.

Diet: It feeds on a variety of animals that it finds in trees and shrubs, including birds and chameleons (kuh-MEEL-yuns), a type of lizard.

Behavior and reproduction: Active during the day, the boomslang hunts for food above the ground in trees and shrubs. This snake, which has rear fangs, will bite and inject venom into prey and into attacking animals. The boomslang is an egg-laying species, and females lay about twelve eggs at a time.

Boomslangs and people: If the boomslang feels threatened, it may bite a person and inject its venom. The venom can be deadly to humans.

Conservation status: This species is not endangered or threatened.

Common garter snake *(Thamnophis sirtalis)*

COMMON GARTER SNAKE
Thamnophis sirtalis

Physical characteristics: The common garter is a somewhat thin snake that may be brown, greenish, or red and may have blackish blotches. Garters usually have three long stripes running from top to bottom: a center stripe that may be almost cream in color and two yellow stripes along the sides of the body. Adults range from about 20 to 28 inches (51 to 71 centimeters) in length, but some can reach more than 4 feet (1.2 meters). Females and males look alike, but females are typically a bit larger than males and have shorter tails. Males' tails make up about 25 percent of the snake's overall length, while female tails make up about 20 percent.

Geographic range: This snake lives in Canada, the United States, and Mexico. Some populations live as far south as Florida and northern

Common gartersnakes eat a variety of animals, including insects, frogs, and small fishes, birds, and mammals. (Illustration by Barbara Duperron. Reproduced by permission.)

Mexico, while others live as far north as Canada and into the southern part of the Northwest Territories.

Habitat: Garters thrive in many habitats, including marshy spots, fields, and forests, especially near water. They also will enter freshwater areas for short periods of time.

Diet: Active during the day, garters eat a variety of animals, including insects, frogs, and small fishes, birds, and mammals.

Behavior and reproduction: Common garters that live in warm southern climates are active all year long. Those that live in the north hibernate during the coldest months. Hibernating males become active a bit earlier in the spring than the females, and mating occurs almost as soon as the females awaken. Females give birth to about ten to fifteen live young.

Common garter snakes and people: Most people know the garter as the snake seen in a garden. In fact, some people call it a "garden snake," and unfortunately many kill these harmless animals. These snakes may also die from encounters with cats and dogs, cars, and lawn mowers. Garters are common pets.

Conservation status: The IUCN does not consider this snake species to be threatened. The U.S. Fish and Wildlife Service lists one subspecies, called the San Francisco garter snake, as Endangered. The danger for this subspecies comes from loss of its habitat. A subspecies is a small group within a species that typically lives in a particular area and usually has a slightly different look from the rest of the animals in the species. ■

Milksnake (*Lampropeltis triangulum*)

MILKSNAKE
Lampropeltis triangulum

Physical characteristics: Although all milksnakes have smooth, shiny scales, they can look quite different from one region to the next. Some have large red or brown blotches that are often lined in black on a gray to tan background; others have bands of red, black, and yellow or white. A few are solid black. Adults range from 20 to 60 inches (51 to 152 centimeters) in length.

Although the milksnake is not dangerous, people often kill it because it defends itself by shaking its tail, striking, and biting, the type of behavior that can make people think that it is a dangerous rattlesnake. (Illustration by Barbara Duperron. Reproduced by permission.)

Geographic range: The milksnake lives in North America, Central America, and South America. They make their homes throughout much of the New World, from southeastern Canada through all but the far western United States, into Mexico, Central America, and south to Ecuador and northern Venezuela.

Habitat: Milksnakes are common in forests and fields and sometimes live on rocky hillsides.

Diet: Young snakes seem to prefer eating other snakes, but adults round out their diet with small mammals, lizards, and bird and reptile eggs. A milksnake typically kills mammals and lizards by constriction (kun-STRIK-shun), which means that it coils its body around the prey animal and squeezes it to death.

Behavior and reproduction: The milksnake is a secretive animal during the day and usually stays under the bark of a tree, beneath boards, or in other small hiding places. It becomes active at night, when it feeds. Cold-climate milksnakes hibernate during the winter, often in groups. They mate in the spring. Females lay about ten eggs at a time, and the eggs hatch in one and a half to two months. When they reach three to four years of age, the young snakes are old enough to reproduce, or have their own young.

Milksnakes and people: Although the milksnake is not dangerous, people often kill it because it defends itself by shaking its tail, striking, and biting, the type of behavior that can make people think that it is a dangerous rattlesnake. Because the snake is sometimes found in barns, people at one time had the mistaken idea that it milked cows, and so they named it the milksnake. It is sometimes collected for the pet trade.

Conservation status: The milksnake is not endangered or threatened. ■

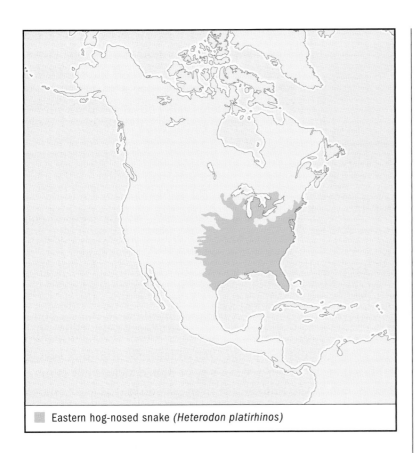

Eastern hog-nosed snake (*Heterodon platirhinos*)

EASTERN HOG-NOSED SNAKE
Heterodon platirhinos

Physical characteristics: The eastern hog-nosed snake has a thick body and a wide head with an upward-curving snout, or nose area. Its scales form ridges, or raised areas, and the snake's back usually is covered with brown spots scattered over a yellowish, orangey, gray, or olive green background. The spots, however, may be faded or missing entirely. Occasionally, a snake may be completely black. Adults are typically about 30 inches (76 centimeters) long, but they can grow to more than 45 inches (114 centimeters).

Geographic range: The eastern hog-nosed snake is found in Canada and the United States. It lives throughout most of the eastern half of the United States and into southern Ontario, Canada.

Some people call this snake a hissing adder, puff adder, or spread adder, because it spreads out its neck as a cobra does and makes loud hissing noises when threatened. (Illustration by Barbara Duperron. Reproduced by permission.)

Habitat: This snake likes drier areas, including fields and forests.

Diet: Eastern hog-nosed snakes eat mainly toads, but they will also sometimes eat frogs, salamanders, and small mammals. Toads will often puff up their bodies with air to protect themselves from attackers, but hog-nosed snakes have long rear fangs that puncture and help deflate the toads in much the same way that a pin lets the air out of a balloon.

Behavior and reproduction: Some people call this snake a hissing adder, puff adder, or spread adder, because it spreads out its neck as a cobra does and makes loud hissing noises when threatened. If these defense moves fail, the snake may strike at the attacker, but almost always with its mouth closed. It does not actually bite. If necessary, the snake may follow up by vomiting, smearing its own waste over its body, or going into a squirming fit. As a last resort, it will roll onto its back, open its mouth with its tongue dragging, and play dead. If the attacker turns the snake onto its belly, it will promptly roll onto its back again as if it can play dead only when it is upside down. Once the attacker leaves, the snake turns over and scoots away.

This is an egg-laying snake. Females usually lay about twenty eggs at a time, although some lay up to sixty.

Eastern hog-nosed snakes and people: People frequently mistake this harmless snake for a venomous snake and kill it.

Conservation status: The eastern hog-nosed snake is not endangered or threatened. ■

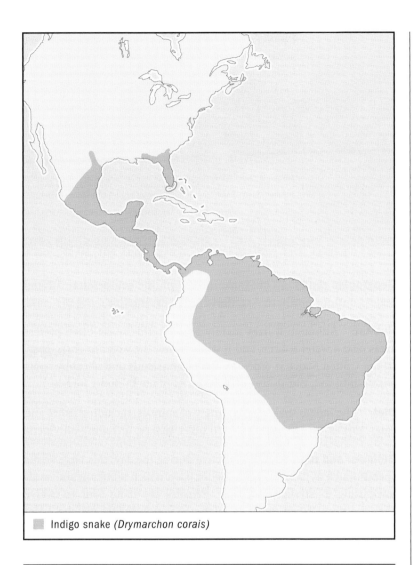

Indigo snake (*Drymarchon corais*)

INDIGO SNAKE
Drymarchon corais

Physical characteristics: The indigo snakes that live in the southeastern United States are shiny black or bluish-black with a reddish throat. In tropical areas, their colors range from black to brown, gray, or yellow. Sometimes, the tail is a different color from the rest of the body. The longest snake in the United States, adults can reach nearly 10 feet (3 meters) long.

Class: Reptilia

Order: Squamata

Family: Elapidae

Number of species: More than 300
species

family

phylum

class

subclass

order

monotypic order

suborder

▲ family

PHYSICAL CHARACTERISTICS

The cobras, kraits (KRYTS), sea snakes, death adders, and other members of this family are venomous (VEH-nuh-mus), or poisonous, snakes that vary in length from just 7 inches (17.8 centimeters) to 16 feet, 8 inches (5 meters). Despite their many differences, all of the snakes in this family, known as elapids (EH-luh-puds), are alike in some ways. They each have two "fixed" fangs, or long, pointed teeth that cannot move, at the front of the mouth. These short fangs are always pointed downward and ready to inject venom. Elapids are mostly thin snakes with heads that are about the same size around as their necks and with large scoots, or scales, down the back. Many cobras are well known for their ability to spread out their necks into a sort of hood.

Some elapids are brightly colored; others are not. Some have stripes, but others are just one color. Still others have side-to-side bands of color. The coral snakes, for example, often have bright bands of different colors.

GEOGRAPHIC RANGE

The elapids live in Africa, Asia, Australia, the United States and Mexico, Central America, South America, and the Pacific and Indian Oceans.

HABITAT

This large family has species that can live in almost any habitat, from deserts and dry grasslands to rainforests and even oceans. Most of the three hundred species, or types of snakes, in this family live on the ground, but some elapids spend at least part of their time underground, and others live nearly their entire lives in trees or underwater. Some scientists split this family into two: the Elapidae encompassing all of the land-living species and a second family, known as the Hydrophiidae, containing the snakes that live in water.

DIET

Elapids eat small mammals, birds, snakes, lizards, frogs, and fishes. Many of them feed on whatever they can find, while others eat only one or two different items. The favorite food of the southern African Rinkhal's cobra, for instance, is toads. Sea snakes find their meals in the coral reefs where most of them live, and they eat mainly fishes, eels, or squids. Most species in this family actively hunt for food, slithering or swimming up to prey, an animal they intend to eat, and then striking at them and biting them with their fangs. The fangs release venom, or poison, which slows down the prey's heartbeat and breathing, making the animal easy to eat. Rather than finding prey, the Australian death adder lets prey come to it. The adder sits still, wriggling only the tip of its tail, which looks much like an insect grub, the very young form of an insect. As the animals come closer to take a bite out of the tasty "grub," the snake strikes.

BEHAVIOR AND REPRODUCTION

One of the most common myths about elapids is that they can be "charmed," or controlled through playing music. Film clips show snake charmers playing the flute and cobras rising from their baskets because they have been "hypnotized," or put into a trance, by the music. Actually, cobras cannot even hear music. Like all elapids, they can hear low sounds, like the vibrations (vie-BRAY-shuns) made by a person stomping on the ground, but they cannot hear musical notes, which are much

SNAKE COPYCATS

Nature is filled with copycat animals, and snakes are no exception. The coral snake is one example. These snakes have powerful venom and, with one bite, can sicken and often kill attacking animals. They also have bold red, black, and yellow bands, and predators learn to avoid snakes with those patterns. There are other snakes that live among the coral snakes but lack their venom. Many of them are colored very much like the coral snakes. While these "copycats" pose little danger to other animals, predators avoid them because they look so much like coral snakes. These copycats, known as mimics (MIM-iks), can be quite common. In coral snake habitats, for instance, these mimic species are so common that they actually outnumber true coral snakes by two to one.

higher sounds. The cobra sways back and forth not because it is listening to the musical beat but because it is following the movements of the snake charmer, who is swaying to the music.

Depending on the species, an elapid may be active at sunset and at night or during the daytime. Snakes that live in warm climates stay active all year, but those that live in colder areas, hibernate (HIGH-bur-nayt), or remain inactive, in the winter. During hibernation (high-bur-NAY-shun), the snakes enter a state of deep sleep that helps them survive the cold weather.

Most elapids reproduce in the spring. In general, males fight with one another, and the winners mate with the females. Many elapids lay eggs, but others give birth to live young snakes. The egg-laying females usually place their eggs under a rock or a log or in some other hiding place. The eggs hatch in about three months. The females that give birth to live young do so in a hiding place. Scientists believe that the king cobras are the only elapids that provide any care for eggs or young. These snakes remain with their eggs and will strike out at anything or anyone who approaches too closely.

COBRAS, KRAITS, SEA SNAKES, THEIR RELATIVES, AND PEOPLE

More than half of the venomous snake species in the world belong to this family, which includes cobras, mambas, coral snakes, land-living kraits, brown snakes, taipans (TY-pans), death adders, sea kraits, and sea snakes. Some of them are quite deadly to humans. Nonetheless, snake charmers and other people annoy the snakes for entertainment or collect them for their skins, which are used for belt and shoe leather.

CONSERVATION STATUS

The World Conservation Union (IUCN) lists seven species as Vulnerable, which means that they face a high risk of extinction in the wild. Two species are Near Threatened, which means they are at risk of being threatened with extinction in the future. Causes for the declines in their numbers may include loss of their habitats, or preferred living areas, and collecting of snakeskins for leather.

North American coral snake (*Micrurus fulvius*)

NORTH AMERICAN CORAL SNAKE
Micrurus fulvius

Physical characteristics: This thin snake has a repeated color pattern of narrow yellow, wide red, and wide black bands. A narrow yellow band separates the black and red bands. Adults normally are 18 to 28 inches (45.7 to 71 centimeters) long, but they have been known to grow to more than 4 feet (1.2 meters).

Geographic range: North American coral snakes live in the United States and Mexico.

Habitat: The North American coral snake lives in many areas, including deserts and forests and even along the shorelines of lakes and ponds.

North American coral snakes often hide under leaves or logs or in some other shelter. (Illustration by Dan Erickson. Reproduced by permission.)

Diet: This snake eats mostly small lizards but sometimes also dines on frogs and other snakes. It tracks the lizards and snakes by following their scents (SENTS), or smells.

Behavior and reproduction: These secretive snakes often hide under leaves or logs or in some other shelter. When a coral snake feels threatened, it sometimes pokes out the end of its tail, which may confuse the attacker into thinking the tail is the head. This can give the coral snake time to get away. Females usually lay fewer than nine eggs at a time, but they can lay as many as thirteen. Little else is known about them.

North American coral snakes and people: The coral snake's venom is strong enough to kill a human, but antivenin (an-tee-VEH-nuhn) is available. Antivenin is a substance that neutralizes a snake's venom, meaning that it causes the venom to have no bad effect.

Conservation status: These snakes are not endangered or threatened. ■

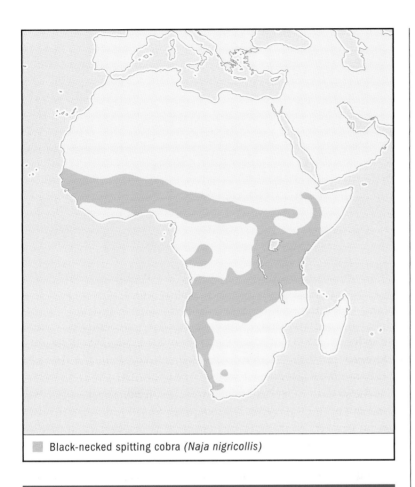

Black-necked spitting cobra (*Naja nigricollis*)

BLACK-NECKED SPITTING COBRA
Naja nigricollis

Physical characteristics: The black-necked spitting cobra may be solid black or brown, or it may be striped with black and white. It has two sharp, thin fangs that it uses to spray its venom. These snakes can reach a length of 79 inches (2 meters).

Geographic range: This snake lives in western, central, and southern Africa.

Habitat: The black-necked spitting cobra usually lives in grasslands, but it sometimes enters villages and cities, where it can cause quite an uproar among human residents, who worry about being poisoned with its venom.

Although it spends much of its time on the ground, the black-necked spitting cobra can easily climb into bushes and trees. (Illustration by Dan Erickson. Reproduced by permission.)

Diet: The black-necked spitting cobra eats almost anything it finds, including frogs and toads, birds and their eggs, and other reptiles.

Behavior and reproduction: Although it spends much of its time on the ground, this cobra can easily climb into bushes and trees. It is most active at night, but it sometimes moves about during the day. Females lay eight to twenty eggs at a time.

Black-necked spitting cobras and people: Local people fear this snake, which can spray venom almost 10 feet (3 meters). The snake aims for the eyes, and the venom can be very painful and can even cause blindness if the person is not treated immediately. A bite from the snake can kill a person.

Conservation status: The black-necked spitting cobra is not endangered or threatened. ■

King cobra (*Ophiophagus hannah*)

KING COBRA
Ophiophagus hannah

Physical characteristics: The king cobras are snakes of many colors; they may be black, brown, brownish-green, or yellow. These large snakes usually reach about 9.8 feet (3 meters) in length, but they can grow to 16.4 feet (5 meters).

Geographic range: The king cobra lives from India through Southeast Asia (the Philippines and into Indonesia).

Habitat: King cobras are animals of the thick jungle and usually prefer to live near water.

Diet: Their main food items are other snakes, including other venomous species.

Behavior and reproduction: Unlike most other members of this family, male and female king cobras will form pairs, make a nest from leaves and dirt in a growth of bamboo, and protect the nest and, later, the eggs from attackers. Once the eggs hatch, the parents leave the nest site, and the young must live on their own immediately.

King cobras and people: When a king cobra bites a person, it can inject a dose of venom that can kill.

Conservation status: The king cobra is not endangered or threatened. ■

Death adder (*Acanthophis antarcticus*)

DEATH ADDER
Acanthophis antarcticus

Physical characteristics: The death adder has a thick body, with bands of light brown to black. Adults are about 20 to 39 inches (0.5 to 1 meter) long.

Geographic range: The death adder is found in Australia.

Habitat: Death adders live in dry areas, including grasslands and deserts, in eastern and southern Australia. It also sometimes wanders into cities.

Diet: The death adder eats mainly small reptiles but also frogs and small mammals.

Behavior and reproduction: Most members of this family actively search out prey to eat, but the death adder buries itself, leaving out just the tip of its tail. The tail tip, which looks like a worm, catches the attention of their prey. When the prey animals get close, the adder strikes. The death adder is a secretive snake and is most active at night. Females give birth to live snakes, instead of laying eggs; they may have up to twenty young at a time.

Death adders and people: The snake's venom is very strong and can kill people. Antivenin is available.

Conservation status: The death adder is not endangered or threatened. ■

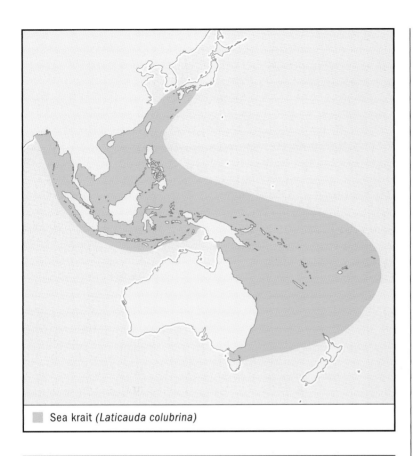

Sea krait (*Laticauda colubrina*)

SEA KRAIT
Laticauda colubrina

Physical characteristics: The sea krait is banded with blue or bluish gray and black and has a paddle-shaped tail to help it swim. It also has valves, or flaps, that can close its nostrils, or nose holes, when it goes underwater. Adults are usually about 39 inches (1 meter) long, but some sea kraits can reach 55 inches (1.4 meters) in length.

Geographic range: The sea krait is found in New Guinea, on many Pacific islands, and from India to Southeast Asia.

Habitat: Sea kraits spend most of their lives in the ocean water, coming ashore only to rest or to lay their eggs. Once in a while, they may travel into mangrove swamps. Mangroves are tropical trees and shrubs that form thick masses along coastlines.

Sea kraits spend most of their lives in the ocean water, coming ashore only to rest or to lay their eggs. (Illustration by Dan Erickson. Reproduced by permission.)

Diet: They usually find their food, primarily eels, in coral reefs.

Behavior and reproduction: Most active at night, the sea krait occasionally looks for food in the daytime. In the breeding season, females leave their saltwater homes to lay up to eighteen eggs at a time on the seashore.

Sea kraits and people: People are rarely bitten by this gentle snake. A sea krait's bite, however, is venomous.

Conservation status: The sea krait is not endangered or threatened.
■

FOR MORE INFORMATION

Books:

Branch, Bill. *Field Guide to Snakes and Other Reptiles of Southern Africa.* Sanibel Island, FL: Ralph Curtis Books, 1998.

Brazaitis, Peter, and Myrna E. Watanabe. *Snakes of the World.* New York: Crescent Books, 1992.

Broadley, Donald G. *FitzSimons' Snakes of Southern Africa.* Johannesburg, South Africa: Jonathan Ball, 1990.

Campbell, Jonathan A., and William W. Lamar. *The Venomous Reptiles of Latin America.* Ithaca, NY: Comstock Publishing Associates, 1989.

Cogger, Harold G. *Reptiles and Amphibians of Australia.* Sydney, Australia: Reed New Holland, 2000.

Creagh, Carson. *Reptiles.* Alexandria, VA: Time-Life Books, 1996.

George, Linda. *Coral Snakes.* Mankato, MN: Capstone Books, 1998.

Lovett, Sarah. *Extremely Weird Snakes.* Santa Fe, NM: John Muir Publications, 1999.

Mattison, Chris. *The Encyclopedia of Snakes.* New York: Facts on File, 1995.

Montgomery, Sy. *The Snake Scientist.* Boston: Houghton Mifflin, 2001.

Spawls, Stephen, and Bill Branch. *The Dangerous Snakes of Africa: Natural History, Species Directory, Venoms, and Snakebite.* Sanibel Island, FL: Ralph Curtis Books, 1995.

Web site:

"King Cobra." NationalGeographic.com. http://www.nationalgeographic .com/kingcobra/index-n.html (accessed on September 9, 2004).

Species List by Biome

CONIFEROUS FOREST
Blind lizard
Boomslang
Common chameleon
Common garter snake
Eastern box turtle
Eastern hog-nosed snake
Florida wormlizard
Flying lizard
Frilled lizard
Green anole
Green python
House gecko
Indigo snake
Milksnake
Neotropical sunbeam snake
North American coral snake
Reticulated python
Texas blind snake
Timber rattlesnake

CONTINENTAL MARGIN
Green seaturtle
Loggerhead turtle

DECIDUOUS FOREST
Agamodon anguliceps
Armored chameleon
Black-headed python

Blackish blind snake
Blind lizard
Boa constrictor
Boomslang
Broad-headed skink
Common chameleon
Common garter snake
Common sunbeam snake
Crocodile tegu
Eastern box turtle
Eastern hog-nosed snake
Florida wormlizard
Flying lizard
Galápagos tortoise
Gila monster
Green python
Indigo snake
Knob-scaled lizard
Komodo dragon
Lesser blind snake
Milksnake
Neotropical sunbeam snake
North American coral snake
Northern Tuatara
Prehensile-tailed skink
Red-tailed pipe snake
Reticulated python
Sand lizard
Southern bromeliad
  woodsnake

Texas alligator lizard
Texas blind snake
Timber rattlesnake
Yellow-margined box turtle

DESERT
Agamodon anguliceps
Boa constrictor
Cape flat lizard
Cape spiny-tailed iguana
Common chameleon
Common chuckwalla
Death adder
Desert night lizard
Desert tortoise
Gila monster
Horned viper
House gecko
Jackson's chameleon
North American coral snake
Sandfish
Southern burrowing asp
Spiny agama
Texas alligator lizard
Texas blind snake
Western banded gecko

GRASSLAND
Bachia bresslaui

Black-headed python
Blackish blind snake
Black-necked spitting cobra
Boa constrictor
Boomslang
Common garter snake
Common sunbeam snake
Death adder
Desert tortoise
Eastern box turtle
Eastern hog-nosed snake
Galápagos tortoise
Gila monster
Indigo snake
Komodo dragon
Lesser blind snake
Milksnake
Nilgiri burrowing snake
Sand lizard
Six-lined racerunner
Southern burrowing asp
Texas alligator lizard
Texas blind snake
Two-legged wormlizard
Western banded gecko

LAKE AND POND
American alligator
American crocodile
Central American river turtle
Common caiman
Common garter snake
Cottonmouth
False coral snake
Green anaconda
Helmeted turtle
Little file snake
Matamata
Nile crocodile
North American coral snake
Painted turtle
Pig-nose turtle
Reticulated python

Snapping turtle
Spiny softshell
Stinkpot
Yellow-margined box turtle

OCEAN
Green seaturtle
Leatherback seaturtle
Little file snake
Loggerhead turtle
Sea krait

RAINFOREST
Black-headed bushmaster
Black-headed python
Blind lizard
Boa constrictor
Crocodile monitor
Emerald tree boa
False coral snake
Flying lizard
Green python
House gecko
Jackson's chameleon
King cobra
Lesser blind snake
Neotropical sunbeam snake
Southern bromeliad
  woodsnake
Splitjaw snakes
White-bellied wormlizard
Yellow-margined box turtle

RIVER AND STREAM
American alligator
American crocodile
Big-headed turtle
Central American river turtle
Common caiman
Common garter snake
Cottonmouth
Crocodile tegu

False coral snake
Gharial
Green anaconda
Helmeted turtle
Little file snake
Matamata
Nile crocodile
Painted turtle
Pig-nose turtle
Reticulated python
Snapping turtle
South American river turtle
Spiny softshell
Stinkpot
Yellow-margined box turtle

SEASHORE
Green seaturtle
Loggerhead turtle
Sea krait

UNKNOWN
False blind snake

WETLAND
American alligator
American crocodile
Broad-headed skink
Common caiman
Common garter snake
Cottonmouth
Green anaconda
Helmeted turtle
Komodo dragon
Little file snake
Nile crocodile
Pig-nose turtle
Red-tailed pipe snake
Reticulated python
Sea krait
Snapping turtle

Species List by Geographic Range

AFGHANISTAN
Gharial

ALGERIA
Common chameleon
Horned viper
Sandfish

ANGOLA
Black-necked spitting cobra
Boomslang
Helmeted turtle
Nile crocodile
Southern burrowing asp

ARCTIC OCEAN
Leatherback seaturtle

ARMENIA
White-bellied wormlizard

ATLANTIC OCEAN
Green seaturtle
Leatherback seaturtle
Loggerhead turtle

AUSTRALIA
Black-headed python
Blackish blind snake

Death adder
Frilled lizard
Green python
House gecko
Little file snake
Pig-nose turtle

AUSTRIA
Sand lizard

BANGLADESH
House gecko
King cobra
Little file snake
Reticulated python

BELARUS
Sand lizard

BELGIUM
Sand lizard

BELIZE
American crocodile
Boa constrictor
Central American river turtle
Common caiman
Indigo snake

Milksnake
Snapping turtle

BENIN
Boomslang
Helmeted turtle
Nile crocodile

BHUTAN
Gharial
Reticulated python

BOLIVIA
Boa constrictor
False coral snake
South American river turtle
White-bellied wormlizard

BOTSWANA
Boomslang
Helmeted turtle
Spiny agama

BRAZIL
Bachia bresslaui
Boa constrictor
Common caiman
Crocodile tegu

Early blind snake
Emerald tree boa
False coral snake
Green anaconda
Indigo snake
Matamata
South American river turtle
White-bellied wormlizard

BRUNEI
House gecko
King cobra
Little file snake
Red-tailed pipesnake
Reticulated python

BULGARIA
Sand lizard

BURKINA FASO
Black-necked spitting cobra
Boomslang
Helmeted turtle
Nile crocodile

BURUNDI
Black-necked spitting cobra
Boomslang
Helmeted turtle
Nile crocodile

CAMBODIA
Common sunbeam snake
House gecko
King cobra
Little file snake
Red-tailed pipesnake
Reticulated python

CAMEROON
Black-necked spitting cobra
Boomslang
Helmeted turtle
Nile crocodile

CANADA
Common garter snake
Eastern hog-nosed snake
Milksnake
Painted turtle
Snapping turtle
Spiny softshell
Stinkpot
Timber rattlesnake

CENTRAL AFRICAN REPUBLIC
Black-necked spitting cobra
Boomslang
Nile crocodile

CHAD
Boomslang
Sandfish

CHINA
Big-headed turtle
Common sunbeam snake
King cobra
Red-tailed pipesnake
Sand lizard
Yellow-margined box turtle

COLOMBIA
American crocodile
Boa constrictor
Common caiman
Crocodile tegu
Emerald tree boa
False coral snake
Green anaconda
Indigo snake
Matamata
Milksnake
Snapping turtle
South American river turtle
Southern bromeliad
  woodsnake
White-bellied wormlizard

COMOROS
Helmeted turtle

COSTA RICA
American crocodile
Black-headed bushmaster
Common caiman
Indigo snake
Milksnake
Neotropical sunbeam snake
Snapping turtle
Southern bromeliad woodsnake

CUBA
American crocodile
Milksnake
White-bellied wormlizard

CYPRUS
Common chameleon

CZECH REPUBLIC
Sand lizard

DEMOCRATIC REPUBLIC OF THE CONGO
Black-necked spitting cobra
Boomslang
Helmeted turtle
Nile crocodile
Southern burrowing asp

DENMARK
Sand lizard

DJIBOUTI
Boomslang
Helmeted turtle
Horned viper

DOMINICAN REPUBLIC
American crocodile
Milksnake
White-bellied wormlizard

ECUADOR
American crocodile
Common caiman
False coral snake
Galápagos tortoise
Matamata
Milksnake
Snapping turtle

EGYPT
Common chameleon
Horned viper
Sandfish

EL SALVADOR
American crocodile
Boa constrictor
Common caiman
Indigo snake
Milksnake
Neotropical sunbeam snake

EQUATORIAL GUINEA
Boomslang
Helmeted turtle
Nile crocodile

ERITREA
Boomslang
Helmeted turtle
Horned viper
Nile crocodile

ESTONIA
Sand lizard

ETHIOPIA
Agamodon anguliceps
Black-necked spitting cobra
Boomslang
Helmeted turtle
Nile crocodile

FIJI
House gecko

FRANCE
Sand lizard

FRENCH GUIANA
American crocodile
Boa constrictor
Common caiman
Emerald tree boa
False coral snake
Green anaconda
Indigo snake
Matamata
Milksnake
White-bellied wormlizard

GABON
Black-necked spitting cobra
Boomslang
Helmeted turtle
Nile crocodile

GAMBIA
Black-necked spitting cobra
Helmeted turtle
Nile crocodile

GERMANY
Sand lizard

GHANA
Boomslang
Helmeted turtle
Nile crocodile

GREECE
Common chameleon

GUATEMALA
American crocodile
Boa constrictor

Central American river turtle
Common caiman
Indigo snake
Knob-scaled lizard
Milksnake
Neotropical sunbeam snake
Snapping turtle

GUINEA
Black-necked spitting cobra
Boomslang
Helmeted turtle
Nile crocodile

GUINEA-BISSAU
Black-necked spitting cobra
Boomslang
Helmeted turtle
Nile crocodile

GUYANA
American crocodile
Boa constrictor
Common caiman
Emerald tree boa
False coral snake
Green anaconda
Indigo snake
Matamata
Milksnake
White-bellied wormlizard

HAITI
American crocodile
Milksnake
White-bellied wormlizard

HONDURAS
American crocodile
Boa constrictor
Common caiman
Indigo snake
Milksnake

Neotropical sunbeam snake
Snapping turtle

HUNGARY
Sand lizard

INDIA
Gharial
House gecko
King cobra
Little file snake
Nilgiri burrowing snake

INDIAN OCEAN
Green seaturtle
Leatherback seaturtle
Loggerhead turtle
Sea krait

INDONESIA
Blind lizard
Common sunbeam snake
Flying lizard
House gecko
King cobra
Komodo dragon
Little file snake
Red-tailed pipesnake
Reticulated python

IRAQ
Sandfish

ISRAEL
Common chameleon
Horned viper
Sandfish

IVORY COAST
Boomslang
Helmeted turtle
Nile crocodile

JAMAICA
American crocodile
Milksnake

JORDAN
Common chameleon
Horned viper
Sandfish

KENYA
Black-necked spitting cobra
Boomslang
Helmeted turtle
Jackson's chameleon
Nile crocodile

LAOS
Big-headed turtle
Common sunbeam snake
House gecko
King cobra
Red-tailed pipesnake
Reticulated python

LATVIA
Sand lizard

LEBANON
Common chameleon
Sandfish

LESOTHO
Boomslang
Helmeted turtle

LIBERIA
Boomslang
Helmeted turtle
Nile crocodile

LIBYA
Common chameleon
Horned viper
Sandfish

LITHUANIA
Sand lizard

LUXEMBOURG
Sand lizard

MACEDONIA
Sand lizard

MADAGASCAR
Armored chameleon
Helmeted turtle
House gecko
Nile crocodile

MALAWI
Boomslang
Helmeted turtle
Nile crocodile

MALAYSIA
Blind lizard
Common sunbeam snake
False blind snake
House gecko
King cobra
Little file snake
Red-tailed pipesnake
Reticulated python

MALI
Boomslang
Nile crocodile
Sandfish

MALTA
Common chameleon

MAURITANIA
Horned viper
Sandfish

MAURITIUS
Splitjaw snake

MEXICO
American crocodile
Boa constrictor
Cape spinytail iguana
Central American river turtle
Common caiman
Common chuckwalla
Desert night lizard
Desert tortoise
Eastern box turtle
Gila monster
Green anole
House gecko
Indigo snake
Knob-scaled lizard
Milksnake
Neotropical sunbeam snake
North American coral snake
Six-lined racerunner
Snapping turtle
Spiny softshell
Texas alligator lizard
Texas blind snake
Two-legged wormlizard
Western banded gecko

MOLDOVA
Sand lizard

MOROCCO
Common chameleon
Horned viper

MOZAMBIQUE
Boomslang
Helmeted turtle
Nile crocodile
Southern burrowing asp

MYANMAR
Big-headed turtle
Common sunbeam snake

House gecko
King cobra
Little file snake
Red-tailed pipesnake
Reticulated python

NAMIBIA
Black-necked spitting cobra
Boomslang
Helmeted turtle
Southern burrowing asp
Spiny agama

NEPAL
Gharial
King cobra

NETHERLANDS
Sand lizard

NEW ZEALAND
Tuatara

NICARAGUA
American crocodile
Boa constrictor
Common caiman
Indigo snake
Milksnake
Neotropical sunbeam snake
Snapping turtle
Southern bromeliad
  woodsnake

NIGER
Black-necked spitting cobra
Boomslang
Sandfish

NIGERIA
Black-necked spitting cobra
Boomslang
Helmeted turtle
Nile crocodile

PACIFIC OCEAN
Green seaturtle
Leatherback seaturtle
Loggerhead turtle
Sea krait

PAKISTAN
Gharial

PANAMA
American crocodile
Black-headed bushmaster
Boa constrictor
Common caiman
Indigo snake
Snapping turtle
Southern bromeliad
  woodsnake

PAPUA NEW GUINEA
Blind lizard
Crocodile monitor
Frilled lizard
Green python
House gecko
Little file snake
Pig-nose turtle

PARAGUAY
Bachia bresslaui
Boa constrictor
Early blind snake
White-bellied wormlizard

PERU
Boa constrictor
Common caiman
False coral snake
South American river turtle

PHILIPPINES
Blind lizard
House gecko
Little file snake
Reticulated python

POLAND
Sand lizard

REPUBLIC OF THE CONGO
Black-necked spitting cobra
Boomslang
Helmeted turtle
Nile crocodile

ROMANIA
Sand lizard

RUSSIA
Sand lizard

RWANDA
Black-necked spitting cobra
Boomslang
Helmeted turtle
Nile crocodile

SAMOA
House gecko

SÃO TOMÉ AND PRÍNCIPE
Helmeted turtle
Nile crocodile

SENEGAL
Black-necked spitting cobra
Helmeted turtle
Nile crocodile
Sandfish

SERBIA AND MONTENEGRO
Sand lizard

SIERRA LEONE
Boomslang
Helmeted turtle
Nile crocodile

SINGAPORE
Common sunbeam snake
False blind snake
House gecko
King cobra
Little file snake
Red-tailed pipesnake
Reticulated python

SLOVAKIA
Sand lizard

SLOVENIA
Sand lizard

SOLOMON ISLANDS
House gecko
Prehensile-tailed skink

SOMALIA
Agamodon anguliceps
Boomslang
Helmeted turtle

SOUTH AFRICA
Black-necked spitting cobra
Boomslang
Cape flat lizard
Helmeted turtle
Southern burrowing asp
Spiny agama

SPAIN
Common chameleon

SRI LANKA
House gecko
Little file snake

SUDAN
Black-necked spitting cobra
Boomslang

Helmeted turtle
Horned viper
Nile crocodile

SURINAME
American crocodile
Boa constrictor
Common caiman
Emerald tree boa
False coral snake
Green anaconda
Indigo snake
Matamata
Milksnake
White-bellied wormlizard

SWAZILAND
Boomslang
Helmeted turtle
Southern burrowing asp

SWEDEN
Sand lizard

SYRIA
Common chameleon
Horned viper
Sandfish

TAIWAN
Yellow-margined box turtle

TANZANIA
Black-necked spitting cobra
Boomslang
Helmeted turtle
Jackson's chameleon
Nile crocodile
Southern burrowing asp

THAILAND
Big-headed turtle

Blind lizard
Common sunbeam snake
House gecko
King cobra
Little file snake
Red-tailed pipesnake
Reticulated python

TIMOR-LESTE
House gecko
Little file snake
Red-tailed pipesnake

TOGO
Boomslang
Helmeted turtle
Nile crocodile

TUNISIA
Common chameleon
Horned viper

TURKEY
Common chameleon

TUVALU
House gecko

UGANDA
Black-necked spitting cobra
Boomslang
Helmeted turtle
Nile crocodile

UKRAINE
Sand lizard

UNITED KINGDOM
Sand lizard

UNITED STATES
American alligator
Broad-headed skink
Common chuckwalla
Common garter snake
Cottonmouth
Desert night lizard
Desert tortoise
Eastern box turtle
Eastern hog-nosed snake
Florida wormlizard
Gila monster
Green anole
House gecko
Indigo snake
Milksnake
North American coral snake
Painted turtle
Six-lined racerunner
Snapping turtle
Spiny softshell
Stinkpot
Texas alligator lizard
Texas blind snake
Timber rattlesnake
Western banded gecko

URUGUAY
Boa constrictor
White-bellied wormlizard

VANUATU
House gecko

VENEZUELA
American crocodile

Boa constrictor
Common caiman
Crocodile tegu
Emerald tree boa
False coral snake
Green anaconda
Indigo snake
Matamata
Milksnake
South American river turtle
White-bellied wormlizard

VIETNAM
Blind lizard
Common sunbeam snake
House gecko
King cobra
Little file snake
Red-tailed pipesnake
Reticulated python

YEMEN
Common chameleon
Helmeted turtle
Horned viper

ZAMBIA
Boomslang
Helmeted turtle
Nile crocodile
Southern burrowing asp

ZIMBABWE
Boomslang
Helmeted turtle
Nile crocodile
Southern burrowing asp

Index

Italic type indicates volume number; **boldface** type indicates entries and their pages; (ill.) indicates illustrations.

Dawn blind snakes. *See* Early blind snakes

Death adders, *2:* 414, 415, 416, 423–24, 423 (ill.), 424 (ill.)

Dermatemydidae. See Central American river turtles

Dermatemys mawii. See Central American river turtles

Dermochelyidae. See Leatherback seaturtles

Dermochelys coriacea. See Leatherback seaturtles

Desert grassland whiptail lizards, *1:* 142; *2:* 236

Desert iguanas, *1:* 168

Desert monitors, *2:* 282

Desert night lizards, *2:* 218–19, 218 (ill.), 219 (ill.)

Desert tortoises, *1:* 92–94, 92 (ill.), 93 (ill.)

Diamond pythons, *2:* 355

Diamondbacked water snakes, *2:* 402

Dibamidae. See Blindskinks

Dibamus bourreti. See Blindskinks

Diet and feces, *1:* 198

Dinosauria. See Dinosaurs

Dinosaurs, *1:* **1–7**

Dispholidus typus. See Boomslangs

DNA of dinosaurs, *1:* 5

Draco volans. See Flying lizards

Dragon lizards, *1:* 140, **145–55**

Dromaeosaurids, *1:* 6

Droppings and diet, *1:* 198

Drymarchon corais. See Indigo snakes

Dusky dwarf boas, *2:* 370

Dusky tropes, Cuban, *2:* 369

Dwarf boas
Cuban black and white, *2:* 369
dusky, *2:* 370
Oaxacan, *2:* 369
Panamanian, *2:* 370

Dwarf geckos. *See* Jaragua lizards

Dwarf pipe snakes. *See* False blind snakes

Dwarf puff adders, *2:* 380

Dwarf pythons. *See* Neotropical sunbeam snakes

E

Earless monitors, *2:* **279–87**

Early blind snakes, *2:* **288–94,** 295

Ears of reptiles, *1:* 209

Earthworms, *1:* 191

Eastern box turtles, *1:* 55–57, 55 (ill.), 56 (ill.)

Eastern coral snakes, *2:* 401

Eastern garter snakes, *1:* 141

Eastern glass lizards, *2:* 262

Eastern hognosed snakes, *2:* 409–10, 409 (ill.), 410 (ill.)

Eastern massasauga rattlesnakes, *2:* 381

Eastern water skinks, *2:* 250

Eastwood's longtailed seps, *2:* 245

Ectothermic animals, *1:* 2
See also specific animals

Eggs of lizards and snakes, *1:* 142

Elapidae, *2:* **414–26**

Elephanttrunk snakes. *See* File snakes

Emerald tree boas, *2:* 348–49, 348 (ill.), 349 (ill.)

Emperor of the flesheating crocodiles, *1:* 103

Emydidae. See New World pond turtles

Endangered species, *2:* 238
See also World Conservation Union (IUCN) Red List of Threatened Species; specific species

Endothermic animals, *1:* 2
See also specific animals

English blind snakes. *See* Blackish blind snakes

Estivation, turtles and, *1:* 65, 96

Eumeces laticeps. See Broadheaded skinks

Eunectes murinus. See Green anacondas

Eurasian pond and river turtles, *1:* **58–63,** 77

Eusuchia, *1:* 114

Exiliboa species, *2:* 370

Extinction, food web and, *2:* 229

Eyelids of lizards, *2:* 251

F

False blind snakes, *2:* **309–13,** 312 (ill.), 313 (ill.), 320

False coral snakes, *2:* 320, **326–30,** 328 (ill.), 329 (ill.)

False gharials, *1:* 101–7, 108–9, **123–31**

False water cobras, *2:* 401

Fiji Island boas, *2:* 343, 344

File snakes, *2:* **375–79**

Finches, Darwin's, *1:* 88

Fish and Wildlife Service (U.S.)
on AfroAmerican river turtles, *1:* 83
on alligators, *1:* 116, 119
on American crocodiles, *1:* 128
on American mud and musk turtles, *1:* 66
on AustraloAmerican sidenecked turtles, *1:* 20
on boas, *2:* 345
on Central American river turtles, *1:* 42
on colubrids, *2:* 402
on crocodiles, *1:* 126, 128, 130–31
on desert tortoises, *1:* 94
on Eurasian pond and river turtles, *1:* 60
on false gharials, *1:* 126

horned, *1:* 167, 169
knobscaled, *2:* 267–72,
271 (ill.), 272 (ill.)
Mexican beaded, *1:* 143;
2: 273–78
microteiid, *2:* 228–34
monitor, *1:* 140, 141;
2: 279–87
night, *2:* 215–20
plated, *2:* 243–48
rock, *2:* 221–27
shorthorned, *1:* 169
tails of, *2:* 223, 244
wall, *2:* 221–27
whiptail, *1:* 142;
2: 235–42
zebratailed, *1:* 168
See also Monitors;
Pygopods; Wormlizards
Loggerhead turtles, *1:* 26,
30–31, 30 (ill.), 31 (ill.)
Longtailed seps, Eastwood's,
2: 245
Loxocemidae. *See* Neotropical
sunbeam snakes
Loxocemus bicolor. See
Neotropical sunbeam snakes

M

Madagascar bigheaded turtles,
1: 72, 82–83
Magdalena river turtles, *1:* 72
Majungatholus atopus, 1: 3
Malayan gharials. *See* False
gharials
Mambas, *2:* 416
Marine iguanas, *1:* 167, 168
Matamatas, *1:* 21–23, 21 (ill.),
22 (ill.)
Megalania prisca, 2: 281
Megalosaurus species, *1:* 4
Merten's water monitors,
2: 280
Mesoamerican river turtles. *See*
Central American river
turtles

Mexican beaded lizards,
1: 143; *2:* **273–78**
Mexican burrowing pythons.
See Neotropical sunbeam
snakes
Mexican giant musk turtles,
1: 64, 66
Microraptor species, *1:* 3
Microteiids, *2:* **228–34**
Micrurus fulvius. See North
American coral snakes
Migration and seaturtles, *1:* 25
Milksnakes, *2:* 401, 407–8,
407 (ill.), 408 (ill.)
Mimics, snakes as, *2:* 415
Moisture and surfacetovolume
ratio, *2:* 297
Mole skinks, bluetail, *2:* 252
Mole vipers. *See* African
burrowing snakes
Molelimbed wormlizards,
1: 191, **197–202,** 204
Mona boas, *2:* 345
Mona Island blind snakes,
2: 305
Monitors, *1:* 141; *2:* **279–87**
See also Earless monitors
Montane alligator lizards,
2: 262
Morelia viridis. See Green
pythons
Moroccan glass lizards, *2:* 260,
261
Mud turtles
African, *1:* 70
American, *1:* 10, **64–69**
Broadley's, *1:* 72
Seychelles, *1:* 72
Music and snakes, *2:* 415–16
Musk turtles, American, *1:* 10,
64–69

N

Naja nigricollis. See
Blacknecked spitting cobras
Names, scientific, *2:* 321
Navassa woodsnakes, *2:* 371

Neotropical sunbeam snakes,
2: **337–41,** 339 (ill.), 340
(ill.)
Neotropical wood turtles,
1: **58–63,** 77
New Guinea snakenecked
turtles, *1:* 19
New World pond turtles,
1: **50–57,** 77
New World pythons. *See*
Neotropical sunbeam snakes
Newman's knobscaled lizards,
2: 268, 269
Night adders, *2:* 382
Night lizards, *2:* **215–20**
Night skinks, *2:* 250
Nile crocodiles, *1:* 101, 103,
124, 129–31, 129 (ill.), 130
(ill.)
Nile monitors, *2:* 280
Nilgiri burrowing snakes, *2:*
317–18, 317 (ill.), 318 (ill.)
North American coral snakes,
2: 417–18, 417 (ill.), 418
(ill.)
Northern ribbon snakes,
2: 401
Northern snakenecked turtles,
1: 20
Northern tuataras, *1:* 132–35,
136–37, 136 (ill.), 137 (ill.)

O

Oaxacan dwarf boas, *2:* 369
Olive ridley seaturtles, *1:* 25,
26
Ophiophagus hannah. See King
cobras
Ornithischia, *1:* 1–2
Ornithomimids, *1:* 4
Oviraptorids, *1:* 5

P

Pacific coast giant musk
turtles, *1:* 66

Stratum corneum, *2:* 304

Striped snakes, *1:* 141

Stripenecked turtles, Chinese, *1:* 59

Stupendemys geographicus, *1:* 82

Sunbeam snakes, *2:* 331–36
    See also Neotropical sunbeam snakes

Surfacetovolume ration and moisture, *2:* 297

T

Tails, lizards, *2:* 223, 244

Taipans, *2:* 416

Tartaruga. *See* South American river turtles

Taylor, Edward H., *2:* 289

Tegus, *2:* 235–42

Teiidae, *2:* 235–42

Terrapene carolina. See Eastern box turtles

Terrapins, *1:* 60

Testudines, *1:* 8–12

Testudinidae. *See* Tortoises

Texas alligator lizards, *2:* 264–65, 264 (ill.), 265 (ill.)

Texas blind snakes, *2:* 299–300, 299 (ill.), 300 (ill.)

Texas thread snakes. *See* Texas blind snakes

Thai water dragons, *1:* 145

Thamnophis sirtalis. See Common garter snakes

Theropods, *1:* 1, 3, 5

Thorny devil lizards, *1:* 146

Thread snakes. *See* Slender blind snakes

Threetoed skinks, *2:* 251

Ticks and turtles, *1:* 71

Timber rattlesnakes, *2:* 388–89, 388 (ill.), 389 (ill.)

Toadheaded lizards, *1:* 147

Tokay geckos, *1:* 179

Tortoises, *1:* 8–12, 87–94

Tortuga aplanada. *See* Central American river turtles

Tortuga blanca. *See* Central American river turtles

Tortuga plana. *See* Central American river turtles

Trachyboa species, *2:* 370, 371

Trawling, seaturtles and, *1:* 25

Tree boas, *2:* 343, 348–49, 348 (ill.), 349 (ill.)

Tree pythons, green. *See* Green pythons

Tree snakes, brown, *2:* 402

Trionychidae. *See* Softshell turtles

Trogonophidae. *See* Spadeheaded wormlizards

Tropidophiidae. *See* Spinejaw snakes; Woodsnakes

Tropidophis species, *2:* 370, 371

Tuataras, *1:* 132–38

Turtles, *1:* 8–12
    African sidenecked, *1:* 70–75, 81
    AfroAmerican river, *1:* 81–86
    age of, *1:* 51
    American mud and musk, *1:* 10, 64–69
    AustraloAmerican sidenecked, *1:* 18–23
    bigheaded, *1:* 72, 76–80, 78 (ill.), 79 (ill.), 82–83
    Central American river, *1:* 39–43, 41 (ill.), 42 (ill.)
    Eurasian pond and river, *1:* 58–63, 77
    leatherback, *1:* 10, 24, 44–49, 47 (ill.), 48 (ill.)
    neotropical wood, *1:* 58–63, 77
    New World pond, *1:* 50–57, 77
    pignose, *1:* 13–17, 16 (ill.), 17 (ill.)
    seaturtles, *1:* 24–32
    snapping, *1:* 10, 33–38, 35 (ill.), 36 (ill.), 77
    softshell, *1:* 8, 10, 95–100

Twig snakes, *2:* 402

Twoheaded snakes. *See* Early blind snakes

Twolegged wormlizards, *1:* 200–202, 200 (ill.), 201 (ill.)

Typhlophis species, *2:* 240

Typhlopidae. *See* Blind snakes

*Typhlops depressicepts, *2:* 302

*Tyrannosaurus rex, *1:* 1, 2, 4

U

Underground species, *2:* 310
    See also specific species

Ungaliophiidae, *2:* 369

Ungaliophis panamensis. See Southern bromeliad woodsnakes

United States Fish and Wildlife Service. *See* Fish and Wildlife Service (U.S.)

Uropeltidae. *See* Shieldtail snakes

*Uropeltis ocellatus, *2:* 315

V

Varanidae. *See* Earless monitors; Goannas; Monitors

Varanus komodoensis. See Komodo dragons

Varanus salvadorii. See Crocodile monitors

Velociraptors, *1:* 5

Viper boas, *2:* 343

Viperidae. *See* Pitvipers; Vipers

Vipers, *2:* 380–92, 399

W

Wall lizards, *2:* 221–27

Walls, walking up, *1:* 179

Wart snakes. *See* File snakes

Water boas. *See* Green anacondas

Water cobras, false, *2:* 401

Water dragons, *1:* 145, 146